AF597252

Books, Balls, & Squirrel Paws

By Mike Rodgers

Edited by Lloyd Culbertson

Published by Yaskey Productions. LLC

Acknowledgments and Thanks

Writing "Books, Balls, & Squirrel Paws" has been a deeply personal and joyful journey, and I would like to express my heartfelt gratitude to everyone who made this book possible.

To those mentioned within these pages—your stories, impact, and the memories you helped create have shaped not only my life but also the lives of countless students. Thank you for your inspiration, friendship, and resilience throughout our shared journey. Your spirit will forever resonate within these words.

To the many incredible educators who aren't named specifically here—teachers whose dedication, kindness, and innovation paved the way for students every single day—thank you. You taught lessons far beyond the classroom, and your commitment continues to ripple across generations.

A special thank you goes to the many people working behind the scenes who often go unnoticed yet remain essential pillars of every school's success. To the school administrators, office personnel, nurses, janitors, cafeteria workers, bus drivers, and everyone who works tirelessly so that schools can run smoothly and be safe, welcoming spaces for children—you have my deepest appreciation. Your contributions, large and small, make all the difference.

Thank you for everything you do, seen and unseen, for our children and communities.

With heartfelt appreciation,
Mike Rodgers

Introduction

This past year, I have been thinking of many stories from my school career. It made me think that maybe there are enough interesting things to be a book.

Some of you may know I have written a few books before this one. At the risk of alienating you already or alternating your opinion of me, I will let you know that the six books that I have written previously have all been about pro wrestling.

Pro wrestling has been a passion of mine since I first laid eyes on it. So much so that I studied the history and roots of this strange entertainment.

Wrestling is something that I like, but being a teacher is who I am.

These stories are about what it is like inside the walls of a school. They started out as funny stories, but that isn't the only thing that takes place in a school. Soon, I was including very poignant stories.

So, just like in school, you might laugh, you might cry. You might feel memories rekindled from your own school days.

From my sophomore year in high school, I knew I wanted to be a teacher. Being an average student, my 8-year college career took a lot longer than usual. The journey was worth it, as I can't imagine what other job or career I would have.

Whenever I was asked what my profession was, I always had a very proud feeling when I said I was a teacher. A friend once told me that I light up when I talk about school and being a teacher. Another friend was kind enough to say I made a difference to many.

I speculated that I taught approximately 8,000 students during my career. I was bound to reach a few!

My grandmas used to write me while I was in college. I would open her letter and go right to the closing. It was the same every time. "Work hard but find time to have some fun." That resonated with me so much. I think I found the job that fits this advice to the tee.

So come on in, we have lots of stories. Grab your seat, the bell is about to ring, and you don't want to be late!

My Journey

Whenever I read a biography and you start at the beginning, I always feel, "Let's slog through this first part to get to the good stuff." So, hopefully, it's not too painful. Slog away.

Beginning

I was born in Port Angeles, Washington, in 1960. My parents divorced when I was 3 years old, and I then moved to Seaside, Oregon, where my maternal grandparents lived. They ran a motel in Seaside, and we lived in one of the apartments.

We lived there for a few years, and then we bought a house in Seaside, where we lived for several years.

My mom worked in retail, working in Cornets and Newberry's, which were what we used to call dime stores.

She also bathed and clipped dogs as her side hustle. On the weekend, she would often do two or even three dogs. One of her regular dog clients had a brother who was visiting from Ohio.

Would my mom like to meet him?

She did meet him and ended up marrying him. His name was George Stribling.

He was a horse trainer and had a huge farm in Mechanicstown, Ohio. He had a ¼ mile-covered track that could also house horses. He would also train them as well.

We moved to Ohio in early 1969.

Mechanicstown was very rural. My bus ride home took well over an hour. The school did not have a gym or a library, two things that would become very important to me.

They did have a bookmobile that came to our school once every two weeks or so.

It was during this time that I fell in love with reading. Our TV only had two stations, so reading became very important.

At the beginning of my 5th grade year, my stepfather was going to race horses in Laurel, Maryland.

We moved there and lived in a trailer.

I loved school in Maryland. All the kids were friendly. I loved PE class. It was so fun, with many games and activities. There were games that I remember playing that I would play with my classes when I would become a PE teacher.

Halfway through 5th grade, we moved back to Ohio. At the end of 5th grade, my mom divorced, and I moved back to Seaside.

I started 6th grade and would finish school in Seaside.

In 6th grade, I had a PE teacher who was literally the opposite of what a good PE teacher was. He put kids on the spot, belittled kids who did not have skills, and made me dread PE class.

Despite this, as high school came along, I really felt I wanted to be a teacher, specifically a PE teacher.

In high school, I had a wonderful PE teacher. I was his aide for many terms in my junior and senior years.

I remember one incident in his class. We were in the weight room, and he was giving a talk on safety. Suddenly, a kid in the back of the room cried out. He had lifted a free-weight barbell with too much weight on it and broke both of his wrists. One wrist was

Mike with his mom and cousin Jimmie Rodgers, who had a hit single "Honeycomb" and appeared on The Ed Sullivan Show in 1957

obviously broken, and he was holding it with his other hand, which, come to find out later, was also broken.

This gave me a firsthand look at how serious rules and safety are in a Physical Education class.

At the end of this ordeal, I sat with this teacher in his office. I got a sense of the responsibility a teacher has to protect students. My mentor is still alive and remembers this incident.

On a side note, the student who was injured had a brother. The brother one day reminded people what cleansing bodily function you can't do with two hands that have casts on them.

MT. Hood Community College

I started college at Mt. Hood Community College, which had an excellent Physical Education teaching program.

Each term had a different focus and activity. These activities included baseball, football, track, gymnastics, and a few others.

Each term, you would be given a skill to teach in this activity. You would then provide a handout to the class, and when the term was over, you would have a notebook of skills and drills to teach this activity. These notebooks became invaluable in the future for teaching.

The comraderies developed in these classes have provided friends that have lasted for years.

Western Oregon State College

After two years at Mt. Hood, I transferred to Western Oregon State College in Monmouth, Oregon. I went for two years and continued in the Physical Education program.

In my second year, I decided I wanted to play JV basketball for Western Oregon. Now, the reason this is of note is that I had not played basketball past Freshman year in high school. I am also 5'6". I had a lack of experience and height going for me.

I got myself in good shape and made the JV team (or at least I didn't get cut). I proudly scored 4 points during the season.

While I was taking one Physical Education lecture class, the professor provided a nugget of information that proved invaluable for me.

He said, "As PE teachers, you need something else to make you more marketable, be it another subject you can teach, coaching skills, or counseling certification. Something that will make you stand out in interviews."

I took the basic Educational Media class, which was a requirement at Western Oregon. I really enjoyed this class, which introduced me to some of the technology and positions that would be available in schools. This was the introduction class for media specialists or librarians in schools.

Beginning my 5th year of college, I had some girl problems and thought maybe Western Oregon wasn't the place for me at the time.

Portland State University

I put PE on hold, transferred to Portland State, and started taking Educational Media classes to get certified as a librarian. I was taking one or two classes a term and working various jobs, including one at the Multnomah County Library in downtown Portland.

After three years, I had finished this program and completed my student teaching at Laurelhurst Elementary.

Back to Western Oregon

In 1985, I decided to return to Western Oregon and finish my PE degree program there.

Swimming was one of the hardest classes for me because I couldn't swim. PE majors needed Swimming 2 to graduate.

I took Swimming 1 in the fall of 85, and it was evident at the end that I didn't have the skills to enter Swimming 2. To graduate, I only had my practicum and student teaching to complete.

I wrote up every lead-up and skill for every type of swimming stroke and brought it to the Head of the PE Department. I contended that despite not being able to swim myself, I could probably teach swimming. My other argument was whether I could graduate with an asterisk that I should never teach swimming.

One day in the winter, a piece of mail came that told me what classes I needed to take to finish my degree. Swimming 2 was crossed off along with the other classes I had taken in the fall.

I never knew if it was a work-study student's mistake, if the PE department had intervened, or if it was just luck, and I never asked. I did hold my breath until I had my diploma, thinking they were going to make me go back and take Swimming 2.

I would like to mention that in my teaching career, I never taught swimming.

I finished my student teaching in Dallas, Oregon, and graduated in 1986.

I didn't need Swimming 2 after all!

Interviews

Holding my diploma and transcripts, which featured 8 years of my college career, I was ready to get a job.

Remember when I mentioned that my college professor said that PE teachers needed something else, especially in the late 1980s?

A job came up in Eastern Oregon for a Physical Education job. A small eastern Oregon town wasn't the job I coveted the most, but I did apply. I soon discovered that about 150 other people also applied for this job. I'm sure my 8 years of an average college career weeded me out quickly.

I did start to get interviews, and they were all for media specialist jobs. Over the next two years, I believe I had seven interviews, all for media.

One interview remains memorable especially with librarians and book banning so much in the news recently.

My college professors in library science pounded one fact into their classes over any other. If a book is challenged as not suitable for a particular age group, make sure that it goes through the proper procedures, they chanted.

They also urged the book to go back on the shelves until its fate had been determined. Kind of like innocent until proven guilty for books.

I interviewed for the library job at Gaston Middle School. The question came up about a challenged book and the procedures. I was ready for the answer to this question because surely all of education was on the same page with this topic.

I replied that, first, I would return this book to the shelves, and then we would go through the proper channels, just like my professors had mentioned. I could just imagine them smiling at my answer.

Upon my rejection call, I managed to ask the principal what I could have done better? He replied, "This was his school and his library, and if he wanted to remove a book from the library, he would."

I realized that different points of view might make me alter the answer to this question in the future, despite what my professors said.

By this time, I had subbed for two years, and the new school year was rapidly approaching. I was ready for a regular job and hoped that I wouldn't have to sub for one more year.

Then, I had the interview that I had been waiting for. This job was for two schools in the Gresham Barlow School District, each were half time. Living in the Gresham area, this was obviously ideal.

I interviewed, and towards the end, they asked if there was anything I wanted to add. Probably sounding a little desperate, I said, "I know I can teach! I know there are a lot of things that I will need to learn, but I know I can teach."

There is one other thing that I believe I had in my favor. It certainly wasn't experience. I think being a 28-year-old male in a primarily female position helped me immensely. I think my employers looked at this as a positive.

It turns out I was hired for one school while another media specialist was hired for the other school.

I Have a Job!

In 1988, I started my teaching career at Hall Elementary School in Gresham. In my second year at Mt. Hood Community College, I watched this school get built. I would spend 19 years of my career in this building.

Working in the Library

School started, and they gave me a week to get settled and get my feet under me. I had to see my schedule and figure out my rules and how they would differ from grade to grade. I got a chance to meet my assistant, who, thank goodness, would set me up for success.

I remember there was a company that loaned animals to schools. You could keep the animals for a short length of time. They had a variety of animals, and I wanted to incorporate them into the library.

The most unique animal they had was Pokey the Porcupine. He came in a big rolling cage for a home. I really thought this was great for the kids because it was rare to see a porcupine so closeup.

I remember we all gathered around the cage, and I read *A Porcupine Named Fluffy*.

Frankly, old-school library classes can be boring. Some of my college classes were beyond boring. I remember one class in which we dissected a card catalog card for nearly three hours.

I had to try to find a way to make the class interesting and still teach these skills. I told the kids that the goal was for them to be able to find the books and materials they wanted, even if no one was there to help them.

One of the most successful 5th-grade lessons I taught was a relay race. Students had laminated book spines with the call number on them (the Dewey Decimal System). They were to find where this book would be if we had it in the library. They liked the idea of getting better at the skill when competition was thrown in.

Another lesson they loved was a scavenger hunt. They were given a clue sheet. When they found the answer to a clue, there would be a letter hiding for them. The idea was to spell out the answer to the scavenger hunt. Again, a fun way to get them thinking about where things are in the library.

Another very popular activity we did was library jeopardy. This involved answering random questions about the library. It was easily the students' favorite activity.

What really sustained students' enjoyment of the library was the books. I always tried to find books with humor because that would appeal to all students.

My favorite book was Jon Scieszka's Stinky Cheeseman and Other Fairly Stupid Tales. I had just read this book to twenty classes, and I had a chance to see Scieszka at an Author event. It was like a night out at comedy. I had just read this book twenty times, and I was laughing out loud as he shared stories from the book.

Another book I shared with 5th graders was Fly Away Home by Eve Bunting. It was about a father and son who were homeless and living in an airport, well before homelessness was so prevalent in our world.

I had never had a book that was so powerful, that when I finished there was that moment of silence when everyone was just thinking. I remember thinking every time, "I've got them"!

With 4th graders, I always tried to show different types of fiction, including Historical Fiction. The example I used was Sign of the Beaver by Elizabeth George Speare.

My example of Fantasy was Tuck Everlasting. In this story, Tuck drinks magical water that lets him live forever. The discussion with one class brought forth a response I remember forty years later.

"Why might it not be good to live forever", I asked? One student said, "You might see all your friends and loved ones pass away. You might be in pain but unable to pass away." That is a pretty deep thought for a ten-year-old.

That first year, I worked half-time at Hall. After Christmas that year, another school opened up a day and a half for their media program. I was hired to teach some media classes at East Gresham.

In my second year, Media went to full-time at Hall.

Mike with another favorite book:
Anansi and the Moss-Covered Rock

The mid-90s brought on severe budget problems for schools. Specialists' jobs were always on the chopping block.

During this time, colleges recognized the need to offer a program for specialists to earn their classroom certification.

Hall's music teacher and I entered one of these programs from Pacific University. We attended school for one full year, which included two summers.

The program made it very easy for student teaching. When a classroom teacher in your building needed a sub, I could be that sub. The school would hire the sub for me. The requirement was ten days of classroom teaching.

At the end of this process, there was a test to complete the requirements. I can't remember the name of this test, but I do remember several things.

Oregon had the highest score requirement in the nation. I took the test and would have passed in any state except Oregon.

This test was like a trivia test. I felt like there was no way to study for the test because virtually anything could be on it. Then, enough people must have complained because the test had just disappeared as a requirement.

I was now a certified classroom teacher!

It turns out those particular budget cuts never came, but I loved having that certification in my back pocket in case it was ever needed.

Hall school had a big population increase. There were so many classes the PE teacher could not teach all of them. The schedule became very flexible, and I was able to teach some PE as well.

I loved the variety of my day where I might teach Library in the morning and PE in the afternoon.

In my last several years, the scheduling became very messy for specialists. The PE teacher and I could not teach the full slate of classes. The school had to bring in another PE teacher and another Media Specialist to complete the schedule.

After ten years of teaching at Hall, media specialists were going back to half-time, and I was involuntarily transferred to two different schools in the Gresham district.

West Gresham & Hollydale

I was originally transferred to East & West Orient as a PE and Health Teacher, but I put in to be a Media Specialist at these two schools and was transferred there.

I would spend Monday and Tuesday at one school, seeing every class once, and Thursday and Friday at the other school. Wednesdays were spent alternating schools, and I had no classes. They were used for grading papers and doing all the library administrative work.

West Gresham was a very old school that was brimming with pride. The kids were for the most part very good. Hollydale Elementary was fine as well, with good kids.

I spent four years between these two schools.

West Gresham had a very extensive Young Authors Day. Every student completed a writing piece that went through an elaborate, competitive process. The best writing was then given awards.

There was also an author visit on this day. Author visits can really have a wide array of outcomes. You can have authors who really relate well to students. Then, you have authors who are just more comfortable creating their work.

One of my favorite authors was from Seattle, and her name was Nina Laden. She wrote bright, wonderful, colorful books: Private I. Guana, When Pigasso Met Mootisse, Bad, and my favorite, The Night I Followed the Bad Dog.

I had her at West Gresham and later at East Orient. She was not the most famous author, but she interacted wonderfully with the students.

Jim Aylesworth was a famous author. What I remember the most about his visit was he was very late. The classes were marching to the gymnasium for the assembly, and he had not arrived yet. He finally did arrive. I have no idea what we would have done if he were fifteen more minutes late.

Ruth Heller was a wonderful author. My memory of her was she did not handle the students well. Ten minutes into her assembly, she dismissed the kindergartners, much to their dismay (and their teachers). She said, "I thought they had had enough." That may have been the most awkward memory of any author visit.

East Orient

After being a Media Specialist for 14 years, that program was cut from our district. Media Assistants would now run the libraries.

At first, I didn't know if I was going to find a position as a PE teacher or a classroom teacher. Luckily, it worked out, and I got a position at East Orient Elementary as a PE teacher.

The first thing I must talk about is what an awesome school East Orient is. The kids are great, respectful, and eager to learn. I always said that I was sorry when the kids went home.

It took just a little bit of organizing to come up with my curriculum for PE, along with thinking through the transitions and drills.

For the most part, teaching at East Orient was wonderful. There were those students and classes that were challenging. My overall memory from East Orient is very positive.

I remember one 5th grade class. Individually, they were great kids, but they would not participate in or be active in class discussions. When this happens, imagine you are a comedian and just bombing. Then you bomb some more.

In fact, let me talk about getting in front of a class. I always taught elementary school, where you could sometimes bluff them, meaning they would listen no matter what you said most of the time.

I would get this feeling when I was teaching, especially in a classroom. You either have them, or you don't.

You bring a level of respect to the classroom. The students must respect the teacher and what they are saying. If they don't respect you and won't listen, teaching will be twice as hard.

I will admit that I wasn't the best disciplinarian in the school, but I really felt like I could teach. I always felt that if students needed an example for whatever topic we were covering, I could come up with one.

In one class, I taught a creative writing lesson. As I recited my example, I asked students to see what I was saying in their minds and to notice how the words I spoke changed the vision in their heads.

This is how the lesson went.

I have a dog.

I have a black dog.

I have a black dog, his name is Brody.

I have a black dog, his name is Brody, and he is a lab.

I have a black dog, his name is Brody and he is a lab. He is 7 years old.

I have a black dog, his name is Brody and he is a lab. He is 7 years old. One ear goes up, and one goes down.

I have a black dog, his name is Brody and he is a lab. He is 7 years old. One ear goes up, and one goes down. He only has 3 legs.

Then, I would ask students to think of the image in their mind at the beginning and how it changed to the final description. I told them that is the power of words and the power of description.

One year, one of my goals was to become more involved in the school as far as committees and extra duties.

Safety Committee

I was on the safety committee; I was on a committee that looked at students who were eligible for receiving special services and the thought and planning that goes into that. I was also in charge of the student council.

I also helped with the assemblies. It was a very busy time but very rewarding.

After seven years at East Orient, PE was reduced to half-time. This meant that I would be teaching at two different schools, neither of which would be East Orient. I was again being transferred.

North Gresham & Hall

I would be at North Gresham and back to my original school, Hall Elementary. We would teach three weeks at one school and then switch and teach three weeks at the following school.

There were several things about this setup. You were half time at two schools, which meant you were disconnected with both schools.

The other thing about the setup was you had a music teacher partner. While you were teaching PE at one school, the music teacher was teaching music at the other school.

It is natural for elementary students to enjoy PE, and it is not fair to the music teacher to compete with that. I always felt bad when they began teaching. I am sure they heard their share of negative remarks, as students were hoping for PE instead of music.

I enjoyed teaching at North, but it had its challenges. The gym was very small, and it had a tile floor. There was no give in that floor, so when students fell, it was bound to hurt.

For the most part, it was a very supportive staff, and I enjoyed teaching there very much.

Hall School, on the other hand, was a huge challenge. I don't know if it had been this much of a challenge during my previous time there, and I just didn't notice it because it was my first job.

I wasn't sure if I had been spoiled by the students at East Orient or if Hall had just become more challenging.

Hall is in a very low-income area in Gresham. School discipline problems were very prevalent. There was a staff of behavior teachers who would come to classrooms to help deal with problems. Listening over the school's walkie-talkie, you would hear pleas for help from teachers about every five minutes.

Classroom clearing was common. This means that a student had become so disruptive that, for class safety, they needed to leave the area so the behavior specialist could work with the troubled student.

In my 29th year, I needed a hip replacement, and I taught much of my 28th year with crutches. I was urged to take at least a day off a week to help me get by. At the beginning of my 29th year, I stayed out until mid-October. Right before I was to come back, North Gresham was having one of their assemblies.

I came and said hello at the assembly and told the kids I would be back on Monday. Who is lucky enough to have a job and have 500 people cheering that you will be back to work on Monday?

I taught at these two schools for nine years, bouncing back and forth.

I retired in 2018 after 30 years. The following fall, I missed school, so I started volunteering a couple hours a week.

Then, I started subbing a day a week or so just to keep busy. I always choose days that were going to be fun.

My last three days of subbing were just prior to COVID. I subbed for music at East Orient, and since it was music time, PE and the gym were open, so I did PE activities. I had the best three days. Then COVID happened, and I figured it was best to end on those three days.

Discipline

I thought I would combine the discipline stories because some people might think they illuminate some of the problems in school today.

The first few entries are meant to be a story arch.

1974

It is 1974, I am in 8th grade at Broadway Middle School in Seaside, Oregon. I am in PE class getting dressed as class is ending.

A good friend, a bit of a prankster, looked at me with a twinkle in his eye, snapped his towel out into the air, and yelled my name, "RODGERS!" It took me a moment to realize what just happened. Snapping towels meant a paddling from the PE teacher.

Mr. Swanson emerged from his office and said, "Rodgers, come here." Now, in 1974, there was no talking back, and/or I didn't have the skill to advocate for myself.

I got a paddling.

Here we go! (approx 1993)

In my first couple years of teaching, I was one of the few males in the Hall building.

There were times when a teacher would attempt to send a student to the office. Sometimes, they would refuse. The office then several times asked me to retrieve the students and ok'd being physical with the student to get them to the office.

So, those times, I would go and sit by the student and sometimes just try to talk with them. I would start by asking, "What's wrong?" and give them a chance to tell me.

Sometimes, that is all the students needed to tell their side of the story. At any rate, then I would tell the student I was sent down to bring them back to the office and wouldn't they just walk with me.

Most of the time, they would. There were several times I would tell them, "If you don't walk with me, I am supposed to carry you to the office." I would give them a moment to digest that. Then I remember saying, "Here we go."

Several times, I did have to carry them. The difference between the late 80s/early 90s and 30 years later was that the students would stay in the office once they were transported there.

Squirrel Paws (Approx 2010)

In the above story, dated from the early 90's, I detailed how I, at times, was asked to bring students to the office by force.

Now, we have jumped ahead at least 20 years. I was asked to attend a training session on self-defense and restraining techniques for students who would get physical.

As the class began, instruction was given. I had a question and explained my circumstances from years previous. I am sure I was now the oldest person in the room. The teacher looked at me like I was a caveman for remembering that primitive time.

The instructor said, "In no way would that be tolerated in today's school environment." I said, "Ok, I'm just askin'."

We then learned about squirrel paws, which are just a way to deflect the fists of an enraged student who is trying to punch your lights out.

At first, the name Squirrel Paws was funny. Each time we practiced, we would say squirrel paws on each deflection. We then learned some restraining techniques that I really don't think would work.

I have to be honest; squirrel paws were only going to work so many times before you got clobbered.

This training, if nothing else, opened my eyes to how things had changed.

I'm going to Call My Dad! (approx 2016)

This story completes the arch. It was one of my last years of teaching.

I was teaching a 3rd grade PE class, and one student was doing something naughty. I don't remember exactly what, but he needed some redirection. I went to talk to him, and I put my hand on his shoulder as I did so.

He recoiled and said, "Don't touch me! I'm going to tell my dad." I was taken aback, but I just said, "That was fine; in fact, I will call your dad."

I replayed the scenario to my principal, who said, "Yes, call dad. Head this off at the pass." She was supportive.

I called his dad, left a message, and explained the situation.

What a world of difference between my student days and the end of my teaching career.

I am not advocating for the right to wrestle a student to the office. However, students are very well aware of teachers' limitations with discipline.

Bribes

Positive reinforcement has been a trend in education for the past ten years or so. Many schools in the Gresham district have adopted a token system where students earn tokens when they are doing well.

Classes dump the tokens in a big container at the weekly assemblies, and when enough tokens are collected, the school earns a prize of some sort. An extra recess or a popsicle party or something like that.

I was teaching a class at Hall during my last year of teaching. This class would not listen or follow directions, so I called for a behavior specialist.

This teacher came, and the class listened to her because she was the new voice in the room. She told the class that if they listened to her for one minute, they could get a piece of candy.

I was truly shocked. I thanked her for coming to help me. But then I asked her, "Is that really where we are? One minute equals a piece of candy?"

She looked at me very seriously and said, "Yes" That is where we are at."

I had drinks with a retired teacher who expressed her dismay at student behavior in recent years and the trend of essentially rewarding that behavior.

In the school where this teacher worked, there was a trend for students to leave their classes and just run in the hallway. They would not follow directions and just run.

From some of the previous stories in this chapter, we know there isn't much a teacher can do anymore if words don't hold meaning.

Staff members resort to rewarding these students if they stop running with computer time or other appealing activities.

This isn't meant to necessarily condemn that either. It isn't clear what the answer is with the behaviors in school. I haven't been in a school since COVID. I am hearing that behavior is even worse now.

There is always a Story

Often, when I was teaching, I would go visit with a classroom teacher about a certain student who was having behavior problems. Most of the time, the teacher would tell me something about this student that would have me leaving and shaking my head.

I ended up having a thought over and over. There is always a story behind these students' behaviors.

It is always something like, well, Dad is in jail, Grandma had custody, their house burned down, and his shoes are three sizes too small. You leave saying to yourself, no wonder this kid acts that way.

One time, I was collecting frisbees as a 5th-grade class ended. One boy started to take a frisbee out of the bag, and I told him no. We were collecting them, and it was time to go in. Most of the class had gone in; it was just him and me. He started crawling on the ground. I let him crawl for a moment and finally asked him, "Why are you doing that?"

The frankness seemed to embarrass him, so he stood up and, in a moment of sincerity, said, "No one ever tells me No. I just do what I want."

Time out for both of us

One time, there was a 5th grader at East Orient. He was a sharp, street-smart boy. He was naughty and very quick-witted. I was on recess duty, and he had done something that warranted my attention.

I went over, and we started having a discussion that quickly turned heated.

I am not kidding when I mention that this boy was quick-witted and a great candidate for becoming a lawyer. He could make you see his side even if you realized his side was 100% wrong.

As we each advocated our beliefs, I held up my hand and said, "Time out. Let's each take 10 seconds." I don't know if it was brilliant or a clear sign that I was losing this argument, but I just put myself in Time Out.

We stood there awkwardly for 10 seconds, not looking at each other. When ten seconds had passed, I started slowly. However, within another ten seconds, we were back arguing.

Finally, I cut my losses and walked away, telling him to just stop what he was doing.

Karma

At one school, the bleachers were folded in and pushed against the gym wall. For safety reasons, I had a rule that no one would be on top of the bleachers.

One time, this third-grade boy was up there running back and forth. He was new, so I told him I had a rule that no one should be up there and to please get down. Now, he had his naughty bones on. He looked at me and just went running on to the end of the bleachers.

At the end of the bleachers by the door was a railing that separated the bleachers from the doorway. There was a big round pad on that railing for safety, just in case someone crashed into it since this was the gym. Now, this pad wasn't adhered to the railing. It just rolled around the railing.

As this third grader reached the end of the bleachers, I saw what he was going to do; he was going to step off the bleachers and onto this railing.

I shouted out to him again, NO, NO, NO. Don't do that!

He looked me right in the eye and then stepped onto the railing, and the padding immediately spun with his weight. I cannot even describe the action that his body took. It was a full midair summersault, and he landed on his back on the railing.

You could hear the air go out of his body as he lost his breath.

Having little sympathy for him, I stood over him and said, "That's why you need to listen to the teacher."

Meetings

The one thing that drives teachers up the wall is the number of meetings in a school setting. Many meetings are necessary, filled with important information that teachers need to do their jobs.

However, many of the meetings deal with philosophy or "Here is an idea for you to think about."

I guarantee that 100% of teachers would rather be in their classrooms preparing for the following day or dealing with the endless details of teaching.

This section deals with meetings.

Staff Meeting

One time, I was in a staff meeting at East Orient. I was sitting next to a good friend during the meeting. The subject was portfolios (this is not a topic of concern for the PE teacher). I zoned out just a little. My friend next to me asked me a question, and I didn't even have time to reply.

The principal called my name and looked at me expectantly. My mind could not wrap around itself how the topic could have turned so fast. I had no idea what she was asking.

My friend sitting next to me started to quietly giggle.

I had to admit to the principal that I had missed the topic change and had no idea what she was asking. This caused my friend to giggle even more as he covered his face with his hands. Somehow, very quickly, these two professionals had devolved into 4th graders before everyone's eyes.

The principal slightly rolled her eyes (I am sure it was not my imagination) and asked about field day.

I would love to have a replay of that conversation about how it went from portfolios to field day in less than three seconds.

Goal Meeting

I worked at one school where the staff was at great odds with the principal. There were many issues that I didn't fully understand, especially when I was only a half-time employee.

Years later, this particular principal retired and came to one of my schools as an interim short-term principal.

It was towards the end of the year, and we had to schedule a meeting to reflect on the goals that had been set earlier in the year.

I greeted this principal and visited since we had worked together previously. He then started to speak on what he was interested in hearing concerning my goals.

Now, I know I was a PE teacher, but I do have a college education, love trivia, and read a lot.

This principal started talking, and it was almost like he switched to another language. He used a string of big words and linked them together in complex sentences. I had absolutely no idea what he was saying.

I remember the little voice in your head saying to me, "Holy shit, I have no idea, no idea what he is saying." When he finished, he paused and looked at me, expecting a reply.

I paused for a moment and finally just blurted out, "I'm sorry, I have no idea what you just said." I saw him smirk just a little, and then he rephrased it so I could understand.

My thought regarding this exchange was that I found you to be unctuous and sanctimonious.

Beginning of the Year Meetings

School districts are very cognizant of meetings. There are days of the week when students go home early so teachers can have meetings.

Meetings vary from professional philosophy to practical aspects of teaching.

At the beginning of the year, a classroom teacher needs to pay attention to many different aspects. They learn specifics about new students coming in. They set up their room and bring out equipment and supplies that are needed. Some of these supplies may be related to the beginning of school and the time of year.

The curriculum might need to be examined to see if it will be appropriate for this crew. I could go on and on detailing the details of the beginning of the year.

Every year, our school district holds meetings during the workweek to discuss educational philosophies. These meetings are never well-received due to the amount of work teachers have and their limited time.

There was this one time...........Our meeting lasted so long in one school that we had to come back in the morning before convocation, which was scheduled at 8 AM during the pre-student work week.

Convocation

Convocation is a gigantic meeting to kick off the school year. It is held at one of the area's high schools, and everyone in the district attends. It is nice to see friends now at other schools, which is a nice reason to attend.

The speeches and talks that go on and on make it less appealing, especially when teachers are anxious to get to their work.

At times, there have been some very good speakers at convocation. Speakers that rally the staff and make them excited to return to their class.

One hot summer August day, the superintendent took to the stage and proceeded to quote every living human possible. The speech went on and on. People were visibly restless and rolling their eyes, and the auditorium grew hotter and hotter.

There were principals and school board members on the stage behind the superintendent. One principal tried as hard as he could to stay awake and failed repeatedly.

He would come awake with applause and shake his head like he was in total agreement with what was being said. Everyone could see he was falling asleep, and no one blamed him. I felt sorry for him.

Convocation Regret

I have a wonderful friend that I have made during my teaching career. We have so many things in common. She was a library assistant. We had children of the same age, we both had labs, and we shared the same sense of humor. Every day, we had recess duty together and became best friends.

When I didn't teach at the same school I would reach out prior to convocation and ask if she wanted to sit together.

We would make plans, the last row on the left. One time we met up, she gave me a hug and sat down. Two minutes later, I heard her say, "I can't," and she zipped out of the auditorium.

She would get so anxious with so many people in a room that she couldn't handle it, but she gave it a good try, especially for a chance to see each other.

Quitting Time

One day in my early career, I was in a staff meeting. I can't remember the topic, but it was a lively discussion, and ideas and opinions were passionately expressed.

The clock on the wall was one of those that visibly moved every minute with a little jerk. The discussion was nowhere near competition when the clock jerked to 4:00 straight up.

Our union representative, a 5th-grade teacher, stood up, interrupting our principal. "Quitting time," she proclaimed. It was just like Fred Flintstone.

The principal's shoulders drooped as no decision had been reached in this discussion.

I was shocked.

They can do that?

Just call quitting time, and we leave.

Later, I understood how much effort and negotiating for teacher rights that our bargaining team works for. This teacher was just upholding and honoring the provision that said staff meetings may go no later than 4 PM.

Extra-Curricular

Kindergarten Roundup

Every year, schools hold a spring event called Kindergarten Roundup. Students who are about to enter kindergarten get to come to school and learn about it.

One year, a group of kindergartners were being led from place to place by some very responsible 5th graders. They had a chance to see the playground, the cafeteria, and their classroom, and now they were coming to the library, where I would read them a story.

This particular class was getting settled, sitting down, crisscross applesauce on the floor. One of my most responsible 5th-grade students (in fact, a daughter of one of the principals I worked with) sat down right in front of the kindergarten girl that she was leading.

As they were getting settled, I said, "Brittney, I don't think the girl behind you can see." Brittney got a horrified look on her face, and she shook her head back and forth, like how could you say that.

Brittney looked at me, pausing, and cautiously said, "No, she can't."

She paused again, and I looked at her, puzzled.

Finally, Brittney said, "She's Blind."

Dunk Tank

One year, Hall School scheduled a carnival. They were going to have a dunk tank, and I was very excited about this. I had always wanted to have this experience.

The event was scheduled for a Spring evening. The dunk tank was outside. As I climbed into the dunk tank, I realized that I would probably get cold.

So, someone hits the bullseye, and I go down into the water. I quickly realized this is not fun at all, and what have I signed up for?

It was cold when you got dunked. The worst part wasn't falling into the water; it was the sudden jerkiness of your seat leaving you. I finally grabbed onto a bar, and when someone hit the bullseye, I lowered myself into the water. I was so glad when my half-hour was up.

Wheelchair Basketball

This was another thing that I was ready for. Being competitive and loving to play basketball, I thought I would be a natural.

The wheelchair that I sat in was very narrow. I realized that my thighs were rubbing the wheels, making it impossible for me to go anywhere. That really could only mean two things, I was too big for the wheelchair or the option that I liked to believe...the wheelchair was too small for me.

I can't let this story end until I tell you I did hit a shot from the corner while in my chair. RIP CITY.

The only thing left now was Donkey Basketball; I didn't get to do that one.

They Are Famous

I was very lucky to have two world-class athletes as students.

The first was Fred Jones. Jones played in the NBA for seven seasons and won the NBA Dunk contest in 2004.

His dunk was memorable and creative. He had a friend in the stands lob the ball from his seat, it bounced once, and Jones dunked it through. The dunk would not have worked if the toss was not spot on.

Jones moved from Arkansas when he was in 5th grade. He was very popular and very laid back in a confident way. He was quite the contrast because he moved slowly and, like I said, in a laid-back way, but even in 5th grade, there was no doubt that he was going to be an outstanding basketball player.

The second world-class athlete is Ryan Crouser. Crouser is considered the greatest shot putter in history.

Ryan comes from a very athletic track family. He was a very quiet and nice student. He was athletic, tall, and lanky. He didn't fill out until much later.

The fact that he has had so much success and to be considered the best ever in something really blows me away.

There have been other successful students. Obviously, doctors, lawyers, or architects don't get their business reported on in the papers, but I know there have been many other very successful students.

I know of one student who has an album on iTunes, Audrey Edgeley. I also know a student who became superintendent of a school district.

Assembly's

In high school, I was very, painfully shy. I really knew I wanted to be a teacher, but at times, I worried that my shyness would hinder my choice of career.

I remember that any time I had to do a presentation in class with my peers, it was very traumatic. However, it seemed to get better and better and a little easier each time.

When I started teaching, at least with elementary students, I had overcome my shyness. With colleagues. there still was that hesitation of speaking out, but with experience and some success, I got better at that as well.

Eventually, I liked to say that I was just quiet and not shy.

That leadup brings us to assemblies. Most schools in our district have weekly assemblies. During the assemblies, students and classes are recognized, and announcements are made. Sometimes, student talent is showcased, and sometimes, teachers put on skits for students. It is usually a fun and fast-paced time.

When I started at East Orient, the principal asked that the music teacher (Michelle Trappa) and I run the assemblies. I was very reluctant at first, but it seemed to go well. After about a month, I settled into being the MC for the assemblies.

One time, as I stepped to the microphone to begin the assembly, I opened the way that I usually did, "Goooood Morning, East Orient."

I had a moment to think that I was happy to have overcome my shyness because running an assembly was an adrenaline rush.

TAG

When I was at East Orient, I was asked to teach a TAG Unit once. TAG stands for talented and gifted. I had never done that before, but I was chosen because I had Media Specialist experience.

I chose Petey, a book by Ben Mikaelsen. Petey is the story of a man born with cerebral palsy in 1920. During that time period, there was no understanding of this disease, and he was misdiagnosed several times.

The goal of my TAG unit was to talk about empathy and who treated Petey with respect.

At the culmination of the book, the TAG students took a trip to OHSU to visit some students who were having medical difficulties. Our students visited with them and did their best to cheer them up.

This was the first time I had led a field trip. Our counselor accompanied us, and I found the whole experience very rewarding.

Human Development

Every year, at the very end of the year, 4th and 5th grade students have the hygiene/your body lesson. There is a film, and then they can ask questions. Some schools let them write their questions so they can be anonymous.

During my first year, I did this with the PE teacher at Hall. He was cool as a cucumber. He didn't bat an eye at some of the things that were said.

I, on the other hand, was getting the vapors.

"What does $ % #? @ mean", one 4th-grade boy asked? The PE teacher just said, "That's slang, and you can ask your parents exactly what that means."

I had a new hero. I was amazed. That was the perfect answer and the perfect demeanor. I had a role model.

I was in there because I had recently had a son and could lend expertise on childbirth.

If I remember right, the general theme was transgender questions. Remember, this was also 35 years ago.

Another question was posed, and I will summarize, "If you are a boy and transform into a girl and you have sex, what does it feel like?"

"I don't know," snorted the PE teacher. Which, of course, was the only logical answer he could give.

Not My Hair

One time, one of my schools held a school fundraiser. Usually, when schools raise money, school personnel do something as a reward.

I have seen the principals get taped to a wall, pies thrown in their faces, etc.

Now it is probably time to confess my other passion is Pro Wrestling. I have six books that I have written on Pro Wrestling. In Pro Wrestling, one of the ultimate conclusions is for a wrestler to put up his hair.

With that in mind, it seemed like the only thing that I could do was offer my hair if the school earned X amount of dollars.

Of course, they earned the amount. I probably have to say, at this stage in my life and career, getting my head shaved was not a big deal, even to the students. It is not like I had a flowing mane of Fabio's hair. My hair was pretty modest to begin with.

I stepped on the gym floor at an assembly to take my punishment. They had sent us a 5th grader with some clippers that must have cost a quarter at a garage sale.

The 5th grader took the clippers and started. He dug a few trenches in my head until the staff member supervising told him, "Wait until we turn it on."

Finally, the clippers were turned on and it didn't get much better. I started saying profound things like, "Let the clippers do the work," "Am I bleeding?", "That is just a little too hard."

I lost the hair match and was as bald as a cue ball after a little touchup by me. This was better than the dunk tank, but not much!

Mentors

When I was teaching at Hall, I was asked to oversee a mentorship program. In this program, people would volunteer time to spend with a student once a week.

Teachers would give me a heads-up on which students could use a mentor. If I saw a student who I thought would be a good candidate, I would check with their teacher.

I remember several successes with the mentorship program. One student was a 5th-grade Russian student. I found someone who spoke some Russian, and it was a very good fit. This student was quite independent, and the mentor did some out-of-the-box activities. I remember they took an outing on the Max (Portland's light rail train system), and the mentor let the students decide not only where they were going but also how they would get there.

Another great match started as a mix-up. There were these two 4th-grade girls, and they were best friends. One had a normal family life, and the other had a challenging home scene. Originally, I sent the mentor to the wrong girl. Then, when I made the correction, we came up with the best solution that the mentor was willing to take on both girls.

They ended up taking these girls on short weekend trips and made a real connection.

I also tried to get companies to buy into the program. I pitched it to Safeway, which would have an employee come to the school, be a mentor, and still be paid by Safeway. I thought it was a great idea, but I guess Safeway did not.

This program was really a rewarding experience for everyone.

Bloodborne Pathogen Training

One day, a girl had a bloody nose during recess duty. My good friend sent her to the office.

Another girl, hoping to be helpful, asked if she could go up with her to open doors, etc. My friend on duty said, "Sure."

Now, let me interject that teachers and school staff make literally hundreds of split-second decisions every day. This was not my friend's best decision.

By the time these two students got to the office, it looked like they both had been cast in the movie Carrie.

I believe my friend had to rewatch the OSHA video concerning bloodborne pathogens after this.

On Strike

Once, during my teaching career, our district voted to strike. It was later in my career, but I must admit I was very naïve about this situation. I had packed a chair and a couple of books and realized I wasn't getting paid. It still seemed like a change of routine, and initially, I wasn't sad about it.

When I got to school, people were wound tight. There were a lot of rules. Exactly where you could stand and where you could not. We had some signs and we walked back and forth. I guess at least at these initial hours there would be no sitting or reading.

If I remember right, there was some sniping back and forth between the teachers, with small differences of opinion on exactly how this would play out.

Well, luckily for us all, the strike ended in about two hours.

It was not the good time that I was envisioning. It was not lounging in a chair reading Katie Bar the Door by Mike Rodgers. Ha Ha.

Activities

Height and Weight

As a PE teacher, I had what I called fitness cards for every student. Anything that I tested for went on this card.

We also would do their height and weight on the cards. I always thought it was exciting at the end of the year to show students how much they had grown during the year.

There were several things over the years that are memorable about doing height and weight.

Once, a parent called me and was very upset about taking their son's weight. They claimed he had had some bullying issues, and this didn't help at all.

From that time on, I made weight optional. Very few opted out, but it wasn't important enough to require it.

One year, one girl was upset with me for doing weight. However, she did it, but she wasn't happy. She was an average size girl.

She came back in the fall and was very proud to tell me that she had worked hard over the summer, done a lot of swimming, and lost a few pounds.

It was one of the few times a student used it as a motivator, which was never my intention. I always told students it was just for their information.

In one instance, I weighed a first grader, and she weighed about five pounds less in the spring than she did in the fall. Her mom was often in the building, and I found her. I mentioned that I don't know what this means, if anything. Still, it is unusual for students to weigh less in the spring than in the fall; maybe this is information you want to be aware of.

I once had a girl grow 4 inches during the school year.

By the end of 5th grade, there were always a handful of students who were taller than me. One boy was probably 5'10". I almost couldn't get a clear view of exactly how tall he was.

Jeopardy and Trivia

When I was a Media Specialist, one of the most popular activities we had was Library Jeopardy. I had a chalkboard set up and questions prepared. I always saved the questions that I had and would add more and more over the years.

There were always times when you needed a 5-minute activity, whether teaching in a classroom or even in the gym. When I was subbing, I used the trivia questions as a reward.

I thought it was always important to use a variety of topics for trivia: sports, Music, books, popular culture, and general trivia.

I would always throw in some questions like*, In What State is the Kentucky Derby Horse Race run?* Another good one was, *who wrote the Autobiography of Michael Jordan?*

A third-grade teacher once told me, "In general, third-grade boys don't like to read fiction. They love real things like snakes, dinosaurs, drawing, and cars." I would always make sure to have a variety of categories. Everyone seemed to love the trivia.

Hockey

Hockey is one of the activities that I really enjoyed teaching. You must spend time on safety concerns because we don't want anyone hurt, but hockey is a great activity for cardio, hand-eye coordination, and teamwork.

I always spent the first ten minutes talking to students about how playing hockey is like sweeping with a broom. Most of them can relate to that because they have done it before.

We always talk about how the hockey stick should never go above your knees. Many kids will remember on their back swing to keep the stick low, but sometime after they hit the puck, they forget and bring it above their knees.

Teaching hockey gave me important insight. I teach, remind, and cajole students to keep their sticks down. Then I will have a student come in swinging his stick like a golf club. I often stop the game to remind students to keep their stick down and remind the student of this.

The student doing the swinging will often advocate that they did not raise their stick despite my assurances that they did so. They are not being obstinate; they just don't believe they did that.

So here is the insight…I don't believe students have complete understanding or can picture exactly what their body is doing.

For example, adults can go bowling and picture what their bodies are doing. If they throw the ball in the gutter 10 feet from release, many times, they can replay in their mind that their arm had an improper angle.

I don't think students have had the experience or capacity to do that, and I find it fascinating.

Sometimes, I get students that have no interest in playing in a hockey game. I love reaching a compromise with those students.

On the floor, there are always lines or boxes painted for various games. I will stand one of these students on this box and tell them under no circumstances should they move from it. Then I tell them if the puck comes by, sweep at it.

Usually, in a few minutes, the puck does come by, and they take a sweep at it. I always try and make a big deal that now, "They are playing hockey!" I usually get a look from them like I am ridiculous, but also maybe a little gratitude that I compromised for them.

I will never forget this one time at East Orient when a 5th-grade class was playing hockey. This class was one of the best I had ever had in terms of listening, trying, and doing a great job.

We are playing hockey, and the puck is in the corner. This class spaced themselves out on their own. The puck was passed to a free throw, extended to the other side, passed to the other corner, shot, and scored.

I remember it 25 years later because it was perfection: three passes and a score in probably less than three seconds. A professional hockey team could not have done it better.

I literally couldn't believe what I saw (sure, it was a little luck), but it truly was perfect, and I was bouncing off the walls.

Gymnastics

Gymnastics…..Now I am 5'6 "and, even in college, was probably at least 200 lbs. Gymnastics was my least favorite activity to participate in in school because I was not built for it.

In my college gymnastics class, we had to do a floor exercise. I remember it like it was yesterday. Forward roll, backward roll, forward roll, frog stand to almost a headstand, which I had never done before. Nailed it!

It might surprise you that I loved teaching gymnastics. There were always gymnastics students to show examples. I always seemed to be able to give good safety bullet points and give feedback on what students needed to do to improve.

The most important thing I stressed was to tuck your head, not get mixed up, and put your head back. This is part of students' ability to visualize exactly what their bodies are doing.

On the second day of gymnastics, we usually did stunts, and the kids really liked them. They sat back-to-back, hooked their arms, and worked to try to stand up.

Lying flat on their stomachs so the partner's heads are close together, and then put a ball in between them and see if they can stand up.

There were a variety of stunts like this that even students who were not good at gymnastics could perform.

Card Game

I came up with a game that the kids seemed to love. First, I divided the class into six teams, each given a name. They were now in lines at one end of the gym.

At the other end of the gym were approx. 100 cards upside down. Each team would send one player from their team to turn over 1 card.

Each card had a sticker that corresponded with one team. The sticker might be a dog, cat, banana, fish, apple, etc. When the student turned over a card, if the sticker matched the team's name, they could take the card back.

Also on the card was a letter. After a team had found all their cards, they would try to figure out the message their cards would spell out. Usually, the message was something like PE IS FUN. The message had to be changed each time I played with a class.

Sometimes, I had wildcard cards to mix it up. For example, a card might say, "Switch places with the cat's tallest player, or this team must not send anyone for 30 seconds." There were other cards that mixed up the game a little.

Flexibility Box

One of the activities that I really enjoyed was measuring the student's flexibility with the flexibility box.

The box is a wooden box where students put their feet up against and under a wooden ledge that sticks out. On that ledge is a ruler that measures their flexibility.

The students stick their feet flush with the box, don't bend their knees, and reach as far as they can. They get a score based on how far their fingertips reach.

I really liked this activity because it involves working one-on-one with a student, and you get a moment to visit. I have their scores marked down, and many times, when I see if they have improved, I can ask if they are doing something different. Almost every time, they say, "I started dance, gymnastics, or soccer, and we do a lot of stretching."

To be honest, flexibility isn't that important to a youngster. But if they can maintain their flexibility as an adult, it becomes more important then. Who wants to struggle to tie their shoes as a 40-year-old?

I had one other observation about the flexibility box. About three students in my career had bodies so inflexible that they couldn't reach the edge of the box. To put it another way, they couldn't really sit straight up straight; their default position was leaning back.

All three of these students appeared normal physically. There wasn't any discernable reason for their lack of flexibility. The most interesting thing that I noticed is these three students also had severe behavior issues. I once asked other PE teachers if they had ever noticed this, and they claimed they had not.

It was almost like I had stumbled on something that could have been studied to understand the reasoning behind these students' lack of flexibility.

Big Ball

Another of my favorite activities is a game with a gigantic ball. This ball is about 4 ½ feet tall. It looks like a beach ball, but it has a bladder inside.

To play this game, we divide the class into four teams, and each team sits on a line, making a square about half the size of the gym.

Then, one person from each team comes to the middle and sits on a scooter. The object of the game is for the scooter people to kick the ball across any line but their own.

The students sitting on the lines are goalies. This game keeps everyone interested, is a lot of fun, and provides for a lot of laughs.

Scooters

Scooters, I bet everyone has good and horrible memories of PE scooters. The good memories are that they were fun. You could get going fast and glide along the gym floor. It was always exciting when it was scooter day.

One other memory that was probably inevitable with scooters was the pinching of fingers when your scooter tipped. I will bet that 100% of the people reading this will have experienced that feeling.

Scooters now have a guard on the handles. If you reach inside this guard, your fingers won't get pinched when the scooter tips.

Basketball

Basketball was not one of my favorite things to teach despite it being one of my favorite activities to participate in. There are so many different skills in playing a game of basketball that it often proves to be frustrating.

We would practice dribbling and shooting. We would rarely play a game unless it was modified, like sideline basketball.

Book Fair

As librarians, we usually held two book fairs per year at the school. They were a lot of work but lucrative, helping to attract authors or buy more books for the library beyond the book budget.

Often, students would get the rules of a library and the rules of a book fair mixed up.

I would always say the book fair is just like a store. The rules of a store apply just like our bookfair. Like a store, you can't take the books home and pay later.

One memorable time, a student came to make a purchase and handed me a hundred-dollar bill. This was in the early 90s. I questioned him as to whether his parents knew that he had a hundred-dollar bill. He said, "Yes, they knew."

I told him, "Let me make sure, and I will check with them to make sure it is all okay."

Upon calling the parents, I was informed that they had, in fact, not given their son a hundred-dollar bill to make purchases at the book fair.

Dodgeball

Dodgeball was one of my favorite things to do as a student and rest assured, the years have not changed anything. Dodgeball and kinder forms of dodgeball are still favorites.

There is an episode of the Simpsons in which Bart peeks into the PE teacher's plan book, and every grade and every class dodgeball is penciled in. He turns the page to find extreme dodgeball in the plans.

One day, as a dodgeball class was ending, a student turned his back on the game when one last throw came his way. The ball went between his body and his arm and stayed there as he kept walking. I don't think he even realized he had caught the ball.

It was something you might see on the home video shows, and I quickly recreated it for the entire class in case they hadn't seen it. It was just one of those amazing moments.

We always played a certain type of dodgeball called Germ Wars. In this game, you imagine the balls are germs; if they hit you, they make you sick.

Each team has a doctor, and they have a baton. The doctor can give someone who is sick a shot with the baton, and they are back in the game.

The game ends when the doctor is hit.

In old-school dodgeball, you get hit, and you are out until a new game starts. Sometimes, that is a long period of time.

In this form of dodgeball, people who are "sick" are usually only out of the game for a very short while. The goal as a teacher is to keep everyone active as much as possible.

Now, after COVID-19, is the premise of this game politically correct? I'm not sure. It would be something that I would have to discuss with a principal. Maybe someone would have to come up with another scenario using the same playing directions. I guess you wouldn't have to call it anything. This is the way we play dodgeball.

Safety

Dog Bite

Keeping students safe is obviously one of the main concerns of teachers. We are constantly scanning situations that may not be safe.

The worst injury that I saw in my career happened in the very first year I was teaching. It was releasing time, and students, parents, and teachers were gathering outside school doors.

Suddenly, there was a commotion, and I turned and saw a young girl bent over greeting a dog that a parent picking up their student had brought. The dog was on a leash and reportedly had always been a good dog.

The girl had put her face right in the dog's face, and the dog bit her.

Her teacher scooped her up, and I ran with them to open the door. We got her in the health room and started putting pressure on her wounds. It was very scary because her wounds looked severe.

Very quickly, EMTs arrived and took her to the hospital. This was a Friday, and over the weekend, I got a call from the school counselor. The little girl had some surgery, and she would have a scar, but not bad.

I believe she came back to school the following Tuesday, and I couldn't believe it. The work that had been done for her was amazing. She had a tiny scar that I was told faded even more as she grew older.

Oblivious Students

One school I taught in had weekly assemblies, and when they were over, a group of 5th graders would always volunteer to push the bleachers against the wall. This process was always a chore because sometimes the bleachers got a little crooked and wouldn't push in properly.

To combat this, the 5th graders would push them very quickly to try and keep them straight. One time, as they were pushing in the sections of bleachers, a student forgot his coat in the bleachers and went up to retrieve it.

I could see the danger that was about to commence, and I yelled at the students pushing in the bleachers to STOP!

The students were in the zone and didn't hear or acknowledge me. They pushed in the section of bleachers that the student was standing in.

Luckily, he was facing the wall when the bleachers closed on his legs. He fell backward, like hanging on a trapeze. If he had been turned the other way, both of his legs would have been broken.

I lifted his torso to take the torque off his knees. The kids were oblivious, wondering how he got in the bleachers. We pulled the bleachers back out so he could get out. Happy to report he was OK.

My nerves were shot.

Bruises

Every year, teachers undergo training that reminds them they are required to report if there is any hint of abuse. Teachers are encouraged to report and let others do the investigating.

I had one such experience in my career.

This very nice, quiet 5th-grade girl was coming into my PE class from lunch recess. I noticed that she had a lot of yellow and purple bruises on her arm. I asked just out of curiosity, not realizing this was to be a crucial moment for me as a teacher.

She replied that she had done it just now on the playground on the bars. My heart sank knowing that the bruises had not happened at recess on this day. I asked again to be clear, "This happened today?"

"Yes," she replied.

I had the counselor help me through the paperwork.

The story's outcome is that the girl never returned to this school again.

I did what I had to do but often wondered exactly what happened to her and how my actions impacted her.

Sleep Apnea

I guess over the years, I have had a severe case of sleep apnea. The first time I ever noticed it was in high school. I had three PE periods and then a social studies class to finish the day. Several times during that last class, my eyes would shut, and I would get called out for it.

In college, there were several classes, be it the subject matter or the instructor's voice, that put me instantly to sleep.

When I got my job in teaching, I soon discovered that if we had a staff meeting after school, I needed to take a No-Doze at lunchtime to stay awake.

There were several times when I fell asleep while I was reading a book out loud.

Realizing this wasn't normal, I had a sleep test and was told my sleep was being disturbed 63 times an hour or some ridiculous number, and I was prescribed a CPAP machine. This machine saved my life. I really didn't think my tiredness was out of the ordinary until I got the CPAP.

Throwing a Frisbee

Teaching PE can be a dangerous vocation. One nice spring day, everyone was practicing with frisbees. At the end of class, I was launching frisbees well down the field, and students were running to see if they could make the long, long catch.

I am throwing them hard, and one time, I had a very sharp pain in my arm. Right when I did it, I thought, OH NO….I really messed up my arm.

It turns out I tore my bicep. You read that right, I tore my bicep throwing a frisbee. I imagine I should have reported that to the office as being injured on duty. I don't think I could have lived it down. I had also torn my rotator cuff previously, not at school. So, I did have a nice 2-for-1 surgery.

Knocked Out

I was once walking down the hallway in Hall. There was a door that was flush with the wall to a kindergarten classroom. This door rarely, if ever, opened.

One day, I was walking down this hall, close to the wall on the right-hand side.

The next thing I knew, a teacher assistant was checking on me. I am still standing. She had opened the door, and I had walked right into the end of it as it opened.

I had no memory of this. No pain, no injury. I had lost about two seconds of time. I guess I was very briefly knocked out. I was fine.

I just lost those two seconds.

Broken Arms

I have seen a few broken arms during my career. The interesting thing is how different students react. It is normal for students to cry if they break their arm. I have seen students cry very hard, as the pain is obvious.

I have seen a very reserved 5th-grade girl run into the wall while holding her arms out to slow her momentum. She was going too fast, or a miscalculation and her arm couldn't take the force. She cried very reserved.

Then, the real point of this story. There was a tough 3rd grade boy. He was tough-acting in every sense of the word.

I don't remember exactly what he did to break his arm, but it was one of those where there was no doubt his arm was broken.

He started to head to the office. He yelled out to a friend, "Hey, look, I broke my arm." He held his broken arm up with the other hand.

There was not a tear or quiver in his voice. It is just interesting how kids react.

Get Down

One time, I was teaching at Hollydale. I heard students come through a hallway, and they said, "Did you see that teacher?" She was standing on the desks.

Now, this teacher that the students mentioned was pregnant. So, out of curiosity, I wandered over to her classroom and peeked through the window.

There she was, standing on a block of four desks that had been pushed together. I have no doubt she was animated and compelled to teach her little heart out in the moment.

I looked through the window, and our eyes met. I just moved my finger downward...Like, get down...What are you doing? Her shoulders slumped. I knew she was in a moment. I watched her as she climbed down.

Later, I told her the funniest part of the whole thing was that she did what I asked her to do.

Lockdowns

As gun violence became a thing in the United States, I got a firsthand look at a school district's policy about dealing with such a nightmare.

During my time of teaching, all the schools that I taught went to the locked front door.

Several of the schools had a window where the secretary could greet visitors in the vestibule before they got into the school.

Other schools had a buzzing system, so they could see the people entering the school and ask them through an intercom their reason for visiting.

Schools that I worked at had hours and hours of discussion with staff on the protocols for lockdown. Many of the classrooms had small windows at the top of their doors, which were covered with black paper so no one could peek in.

For a while, there was a red or green piece of paper that was to be hung outside the door or placed in the window, indicating whether all students were inside or some were outside the room for whatever reason.

The one thing that was the most disturbing to staff members was the decision that during a lockdown procedure your door had been locked, under no circumstances do you open your door.

Unpacking that protocol means that if a student had been in the restroom when the lockdown call comes, and the door gets locked, staff members do not open the door for that student. They urge them to find a place to hide.

These discussions were very emotional. Teachers claimed that they could not ignore a student knocking on their door, and they were met with the response that they could be endangering the entire class.

There are no right answers to this problem. Each teacher had to start examining their teaching environment, looking for exits and hiding places.

Once, I was instructed to take my students into a basement storage area downstairs from my gym. It was a hiding place, but there were no exits other than how we came in.

Schools have always had monthly fire drills and yearly earthquake drills. Now, several times a year, they have lockdown drills, which are practiced in case of emergency.

It is a terrible thing that schools have to even deal with this situation.

People in School

Student Rapport

I once asked a principal if they knew every student's name in school. She said, "I think so. What about you?" I said, "I think I do, except maybe all the kindergarteners."

It was such a simple question but one that filled me with comradery. I always tried to build rapport with students. I teased them at times, they usually responded.

I had some favorite sayings that I would go to over and over again.

They would tell me they lost a tooth. I would always inquire about the tooth fairy. They would tell me what the tooth fairy had brought. Then I would always make a big deal and ask the student if they wanted me to knock a bunch more teeth out so the tooth fairy would return and they could be rich.

I laugh out loud when I think of the looks that the kids would give me to think a teacher would say something like that to them. They would always laugh or start to move away from me in a silly way.

Another of my favorites, especially when we had basketballs out, was spotting a student I knew I could tease and say, "Hey, if I make this basket, you owe me a dollar."

Sometimes, they would take me seriously, nearly panicked, and say, "I don't have a dollar." I would banter back, "Well, you will have to bring it tomorrow."

Other times, they would buy in, and if I missed, they would say, "Now you owe me a dollar." "Oh No, that's not how this works," I would say.

Whatever silly thing I said, I think it brought the students closer to me so that we could have fun.

Phil Klindt

I have tried not to mention too many names in this book. I am happy to mention this wonderful teacher, and I have several good stories about him.

Phil Klindt passed away in Fall of 2024 and his memorial reminded me of what a good person he was.

Callie

Phil brought his Labrador to school every day. The Lab's name was Callie, and she was so well-trained. She slept behind Phil's desk, and a few times a day, he would tell Callie to go check on things, and she would roam the room. The kids were just used to her being there, and they would reach out absent-mindedly when she walked by to give her a pet.

This teacher had a room that was very far from the office, but he would send Callie to the office to pick up or deliver things.

He would reward kids with Callie time, and Callie would get to spend extra time with them.

I loved it when I would visit with this teacher before school and Callie would always come to me and get some pets.

A Prank on Phil

One time and I don't know the exact story, but I believe our principal played a prank on Phil.

As mentioned above, Phil loved animals, but the prank was that there had been a complaint about him and a story of animal abuse.

A man in uniform came to the school to question Phil on this topic. I remember walking by the counselor's office. It had a window, and you could see inside. I saw Phil looking very serious while talking with this gentleman.

It quickly came out that this was a joke, and Phil was very relieved.

Student to Teacher

This has happened several times: I taught a student, and they grew up, got a job teaching, and became a peer. It makes you feel old, but it is also very gratifying.

One instance of a student that became a peer. I remember she at one time won my sportsmanship award, an award that I give to students who show sportsmanship.

One year, we had a special award for teachers that recognized their hard work. I won this award, and then it was your responsibility to pass along the award.

I thought it fitting that the student who had once won my sportsmanship award as a student win this teacher award as well.

My Favorite Student!

I saw every student in school each year. For several years, I taught in two schools simultaneously. I estimated that I taught 8,000 students during my career.

When asked if I ever had a favorite student, one comes to mind!

I was at East Orient, and this first-grade girl started following me around at recess. I would always visit with students, and then I would usually tell them, "OK, time to go play!"

For some reason, I don't think I said that to this student. She was always smiling and laughing at the silly things I said as we walked around the playground.

She was in this school through 5th grade. Sometimes, students become more aloof as they get older. This student never did, always smiling, laughing, and a genuine greeting.

This one was a talker though! Talk, talk, talk! One time we were in a class discussion, and she continued to talk with friends. I finally was stern with her.

The next day, I saw her and asked, "Are you mad at me?" "No," she laughed, surprised that I would ask that.

The next time I saw her was probably at the end of her high school or early college career. She was working in a school supply store.

I came around the corner, and we almost bumped into each other. She was a very good volleyball player and was now probably about 5 inches taller than me.

I made my purchase and didn't think of anything clever to say, so I went to my car. I decided I needed to say a little more. I went back into the store and told her she was always a favorite of mine, and we laughed a little at the memories.

Several years later, she reached out on Facebook and sent the nicest note. She said an assignment was to reflect on a person she appreciated throughout her schooling who may have influenced her career path.

Well, to be sure, that did make my day, but the story doesn't quite end there.

This favorite student started going out with my great-nephew. They got married and have started a family!

So, out of 8,000 students, my favorite student ended up being my great-niece!

Girls & Boys

The time for a PE class has usually always been 25 minutes. I always like students to be moving the moment they come into the gym.

I usually want directions to be quick, easy, and concise because, again, I want students to move and engage quickly without wasting any time. I consider these when I decide how to set up the class and the transitions that I want.

One time, I had a friend come in to guest teach. He was a golf pro at a local golf course, and he brought mats, plastic golf balls, target nets, and a selection of golf clubs.

This was a 5th-grade class. We had the mats set up so that one set of students would hit towards one wall, and the other set of students would hit towards the other wall.

In this instance, the transition was boys on this side and girls on that side. I chose these directions because, in two sentences, students knew where to go.

I also used these directions because, in 5th grade, boy/girl interaction is starting. Sometimes, the girls don't want to participate in activities as the boys sometimes tease them.

This class's teacher apparently peeked in on their class and later left a note in my box. The note said, "Please don't group students by gender."

I was a little disturbed because, being in the gym, your classroom is open, so everyone can see and second-guess your methods.

I tried to overcome that and think to see if my style and methods were beginning to be outdated.

I spoke with a principal and talked a little about grouping students by gender because generally, students in the upper ages (4th and 5th grade) want to participate with their own gender, and speaking in a generality, girls are usually not as competitive as boys.

My principal said that when you were dividing students into a very competitive game, you could mention that this group is for the competitive people, and this group is for the less competitive people who would like to play more for fun.

In this instance, I would have kept the setup as it was. Directions were quick and concise. If I had grouped students any other way, it would have taken much more time to organize and take away from participation time.

Saying Hello

Several times during my career, I had a duty where I was a door monitor or directing traffic. The door monitor welcomed the students as they entered the building. I would try to say hello to every student.

It is surprising, but sometimes students need to be taught to say Hello. I might tease them after I say Hello. If they don't say anything, I might break into, "Well, Hello, Mr. Rodgers, how are you today?"

It is a gentle way of showing students what to say. Of course, most know what to say, but honestly, there are a few students who just have no idea.

Another duty I had was at East Orient, and it was directing students to the cafeteria during lunchtime. It was a bottleneck of students, and I would only let a few go at a time.

That presented a time when I could visit with almost every student, ask them what they were going to eat today at lunch, or do a little bit of visiting.

The principal was strict and preferred quiet. Several times, she shushed me, to the delight of the students.

Who is That?

In my first year of work at Hall School, the principal had a car accident and had to be replaced by a new principal. The new principal was a gentleman about 60 years of age, who always wore a suit and was very quiet.

A few weeks after he became our principal, I was in my hometown of Seaside, Oregon. I was walking down the street with my young son.

This man who was very casually dressed stepped directly in front of me as to block my way. I looked at him for about 5 seconds, and he looked back at me with no expression. It became very uncomfortable.

Finally, I recognized him as my principal, and he laughed, "You didn't recognize me? Is it because of my clothes?"

I told him I guess so, and it was a different setting. He never let me forget that funny incident.

Prep Time

Music, Library, PE, and computer time are also called prep time for teachers. While the subjects themselves are very valuable, they also provide prep or break time for classroom teachers.

This is a time when teachers prepare materials, use the facilities, and take a moment to breathe. It usually lasts 25 minutes and goes by very fast.

One time, a kindergarten teacher was delivering her class to PE. One student had a meltdown during this time. This teacher could have just passed the student along to me to deal with since I am a real teacher.

Instead, she knew what this student needed and to sooth him, she sat down on the floor and rocked him for almost the entire time of her prep time.

I am impressed with most classroom teachers, but this teacher went above and beyond. This is an example of what the public never sees about our teachers.

Field Day

Field Day

Field day can be one of the best days of the year. However, it is also a day that involves a lot of work and planning.

I have done field day many ways.

The first way I ran field day was by having students sign up for events. They had choices, and they would sign up for several events. The advantage of this was if they didn't want to get wet in the balloon toss, they could do something else.

Another way that I did field day was to have classes rotate through each event. The advantage was that every student got to do every event.

There was one other way we did field day, and you could only do this method at a great school like East Orient. We had all the normal stations open, and then we added a lot of stations, like face painting, coloring, and numerous others.

Then, we let the students go to whatever stations they wanted to. The teachers just wandered around, and it worked great.

We would always finish with the tug-of-war. The kids loved it, and I hated it. There is such an overwhelming feeling of defeat if they lose. Plus, you can mark it down: there will always be at least one injury in the tug-of-war.

One year, I had the rope sitting in the grass, and for some reason, an army of ants gathered on the rope. They were evidently attracted to it. We had to cancel Tug of War that year because it was covered.

I believe I have several field day stories:

It's Early

The very first field day I ever had was at Hall. I had planned the events and collected the equipment, but I didn't know how long it would take me to set it up. Remember, this was my first field day. I would later learn to delegate.

I got to school at a little before 5 AM. I opened the side door that led to the playground. When I opened the door, I nearly had a heart attack. A student was waiting for me.

She didn't miss a beat, "Can I help you set up?"

"Do you know it's 5 O'clock in the morning? Does your family know you are here?'

" Yes," she replied.

I said, " Why don't you come back at 7:30, and you can help me? Go back home and take a nap. It is way too early."

Who does this?

My relationship at Hall for the last few years was not good for some reason.

I put on a field day that ran very well. However, I didn't receive any thanks or words of appreciation from staff or administration.

I did get one, thank you. A 5th-grade boy opened the doors leading out to the field. He came to a stop as he looked out on all the activities. He said, "Who did this? Who organized all of this?" I stood behind him and told him I did. He just looked at me and said, "Thank you."

Sponge Toss

The event that I usually participated in during field day was the sponge toss. I held a board in front of me with a body drawn on it. Then, there was a head hole cut out. I stuck my head through the cutout. The students then had wet sponges they would throw at me, trying to hit me in the face.

This was fun for everyone involved. I really enjoyed doing it because I could tease the students, and they thought the idea was wonderful.

Now and then you had the gentle soul students who didn't really want to throw wet sponges at me, but I urged them it was OK.

Over the years, I have learned quite a bit about this event. You should have a piece of plastic on the ground in front of it. That way, the sponges would not pick up all the dirt and rocks on the ground.

I always wore sunglasses to try and prevent getting water in my eyes. I always had a towel to be able to wipe off. Usually, at the end of the day, I have 500 students throwing at me.

I was tired.

One story I remember is that a 5th-grade boy nailed me in the nose pretty hard with a heavy, wet sponge.

I had to take a quick time out. I pulled my head out of the hole and adjusted my nose. He evidently didn't know I was taking a time out or wanted a better challenge. He threw again; his sponge went through the hole and nailed me again, right in the same spot on my nose and just as hard!

Concepts in School

Movement in Education

There are always trends in education that seem to go around and around.

When I was getting my classroom certification, one of the trends was movement in education. The idea was that movement helped a learner receive information in a different way, a way that might help that person retain the information.

One day, I was being observed by a professor from the college where I was getting my classroom credit. I took a game from PE and applied it to a concept that we were learning.

If I remember correctly, one side of the room was filled with hunters, and the other side was filled with deer. The deer were trying to make it to the other side of the room without getting tagged.

If the deer were tagged, they sat out a round. The deer that made it were still deer and would run again. This time, if a hunter didn't tag a deer, they had to sit out a round.

This showed the concept of supply and demand; if a hunter was unsuccessful, they might have to move or perish due to lack of food.

We went through a few rounds of this, and I checked to ensure we understood what we were trying to show. The kids got it, and I was happy with a successful lesson.

The professor was pleased and talked about movement in education and how this was one of the best examples that he had seen.

Medicating Students

Medicating students has always been controversial with schools and parents. Parents usually resist the idea of medicating their children, and understandably so

As a teacher, I have seen students who could not stand or sit still if they wanted to. They could not stand still for a minute if you promised them a million dollars. Honestly, those students need a little help. A little help to focus and calm their bodies.

I have also seen it go a little too far. In one instance, I noticed a student who almost seemed like he wasn't feeling well. He wasn't his usual outgoing self. I asked if he was feeling okay. He openly complained, "No. They started giving me medicine."

I checked with his teacher, and she confirmed that he did start being medicated that week. I chimed in my 2 cents worth, but it didn't look like they had his dose correct yet.

Competition

I have always been competitive in games and have always done my best. Here is a difference, however. I always wanted to win and tried my best, but winning wasn't that important to me.

I loved to play basketball. Coming from a small town, it was all we could do to get 8 or 10 kids to play. We usually never kept score and just played and played.

When I got to Portland and played basketball, you had to keep score because another group of kids always wanted to play, and you had to win to keep the court.

When we played games in my PE class, we never kept score. I told the kids, "We are always going to do our best and try hard. But we aren't going to worry about who wins and loses. We are just trying to have fun."

That is a tough concept for very competitive kids. There is nothing wrong with that either, but in PE class, where many students are just learning a game or a skill, worrying about winning and losing can take a lot of fun out of the games.

Sometimes, it is obvious who wins in a game. Again, I always try to downplay it.

Grading

I felt that grading for specials was always hard to wrap my head around.

There were usually a limited number of opportunities in library class to do written work to obtain a grade. For 4th and 5th graders, I always had them do one book report over the term. I figured they should be able to read one book.

One year after Christmas break, school started on a Tuesday. The following Monday was a Holiday, and the following Monday was a snow day. Anyway, at the end of the term, I had no written grades for this 3rd-grade class, which was held on Mondays.

I gave everyone pluses or whatever grades were being offered.

Later, the teacher for that class came to me because I had forgotten to write one student's name down when I offered grades for her class.

I had to open my grade book, pretend to stare at the blank page where no grades were written down, and tell her that this student got a plus.

Gradual Entry Kindergarten

Gradual entry kindergarten is a lot of fun. To make their transition easier, kindergarten usually starts with 5 to 7 students per day.

I really enjoy it when these small groups come to the gym. I usually start by having them sit down and then sit down with them.

Then we just start visiting. I ask them what they think of school so far. What has been their favorite thing? Did they eat lunch, and what did they have? I also ask if they have any pets.

Usually, you will get one of two that will feel comfortable and just talk and talk. Others will give you the quiet one- or two-word answers.

Then, I asked them if they knew what PE was and what things we did in the gym. We review some very basic rules, and then I tell them we should play a game.

Then I pick out a really easy game that usually involves tag.

Usually, at the end of their class, they are ready for more fun times in the gym.

Empathy

This is a skill that is very hard to teach to youngsters.

I remember when I was in 6th grade, and at recess, we would play a softball game. We had been playing kickball, in which you would throw the ball at any runners who were not on the base. Of course, a softball is much harder.

During the game, I threw towards second base to try to get a runner out. The ball hit the runner in the head. I laughed and shouted, "He's out!!! He is knocked out!"

I remember being delighted that I made that throw. The duty person scolded me and reminded me of a rule called Cross Out in softball, where you rolled the ball in front of a runner to get them out.

Even now that is a fond memory, so maybe empathy isn't retroactive. I do feel empathy now. There isn't a Grays Anatomy that comes on that I am not sniffling at.

When trying to teach empathy, the most common thing I say is, "How would you feel if someone said that or did that to you?" Sometimes, that does the trick; they recognize the mistake.

Sometimes, they answer that if someone did that to me, I would punch them. Then I ask if the person they wronged should punch them.

If they can't understand this concept, they are just not ready to learn empathy. However, most students will start to understand.

I have one example of empathy that I remember twenty-five years later. One year, my mom passed away one week before spring break. I returned to school just to check on something a day before Spring Break.

There was a 4th-grade class lined up to go into PE class. One girl that I didn't know very well broke from the line and didn't say a word, but she gave me the best hug. It was so heartfelt it really touched me.

March of Dimes

Another example of empathy is that we always participated in The March of Dimes Readathon at Hall. Students asked to get pledges that would be donated to The March Of Dimes.

We saw a video of what March of Dimes was all about and the good that some donations could do. Students would win medallions to honor the money they turned in.

Milestone Moments

Hired

I had interviewed for Hall School and was awaiting the call to see if I had the job. You know when you are young and you just are not detail-oriented? I kept my phone (landline) on the edge of the bed.

Somehow, it had slipped off the bed, between the bed and the wall, and the main part came off the cradle.

Hall School had been calling me to tell me the news. Luckily, they did not give up when they couldn't reach me by phone.

The Principal came to my apartment to tell me the news. Now, once again, you know when you are young and you are not expecting anyone to come to your apartment, and it is a mess.

So, she came in and told me that I now had a job at Hall Elementary. I was torn between embarrassment as I looked around my apartment, and elation of getting a job.

Transferred

I had been at Hall School for ten years. The Principal had been telling the staff that there would be some involuntary transfers.

I had never been through that process before, and I felt that in the position I was in (Media Specialist), it was very unlikely that I would be transferred.

The principal calls me in and tells me that I will be transferred. This Principal is usually friendly and jolly. I notice his hands are shaking almost uncontrollably. I had to ask him to repeat himself as he told me what schools I would be going to.

Then, I made sure to shake his hand. I was touched by how upset the process was making him.

The process was very upsetting to me. This was my first school, and I very much wanted to stay there. Unbeknownst to me, I would be heading to some wonderful schools.

I was Salty

When I was transferred, I was being replaced by a classroom teacher who was not certified as a Media Specialist.

I had nothing against this teacher, but I was very indignant that a non-certified person was being placed in this position. It was a slap in the face to the education and training that I had put in.

To add insult to injury, I was asked to sit down with this person and, in a half-hour meeting, essentially explain how to be a Media Specialist.

Ten minutes into the meeting, I flat-out told her, I'm sorry, but I'm having trouble with this meeting. I am trying to explain my position in half an hour, a position where I had three years of education.

My Last Year at Hall

During my last year at Hall, I arrived at a meeting before anyone else had and mentioned to my Principal that I had turned in my retirement papers.

"Did I want to mention it to the staff?" I really knew very few people on the staff and said, "No, that's ok."

In the meantime, a very young teacher came in and sat at my table and just heard the last part of the conversation.

"Are you having a baby?" the young teacher asked.

"No, I am retiring" (and I wanted to add that I'm 57 years old), I said, shaking my head.

Retiring

The year that I retired, we were getting ready for the last assembly of the year. I imagined that North Gresham might do something to honor me. I knew that I wouldn't be able to speak, so I wrote down my thoughts to hand to someone who could read them.

North Gresham did not disappoint, and they sang, "He's a Jolly Good Fellow," as I tried not to melt down.

Someone with the microphone asked if I wanted to say anything. I passed them the note, and if my memory serves me correctly, this is what it said: *"I have taught for 30 years, many years at two different schools and taught every student in the school. I estimate that I have taught about 8,000 students in my career.*

I can't think of anything else I would rather have done for a career.

(I mentioned this in the intro) *My grandmother used to write me when I was in college. I loved to read the closing of her letters; it always said the same thing; "Work hard and find time to have some fun."*

I take those words of wisdom and tried to put it in my teaching, and I think we did it!"

After this emotional event, I immediately had a class to teach. As I walked to the gym, a class was waiting for me. Several gently teased, "Were you crying, Mr. Rodgers?"

"No, I just had something in my eye," I replied.

"Sure, tears" they yelled!

Miscellaneous

Mr. Rogers

On February 28th, 2003, a mom was driving a student to school. On the way, as they listened to the radio, the announcer relayed the news that Mr. Rogers (Fred Rogers) had passed away.

The student suddenly burst into tears. It took mom a moment to realize what was wrong.

She quickly told him it was the Mr. Rogers on TV and not the Mr. Rodgers at school.

Two Generations

One time, about fifteen years into my career, I was teaching at East Orient. A mom came up to me with a smile on her face and said, "Mr. Rodgers?"

I said, "Yes," and I had a funny feeling. She said, "You were my PE teacher, and now you are going to be my daughters."

That was interesting and a little startling.

That happened several times over my career. I knew I had to retire because the chances of teaching a third generation were increasing.

Batman

When I was at North Gresham, a special needs student carried a plush stuffed Batman with him. He carried it with him everywhere for months and months.

One day, there was a school-wide email asking everyone if they had seen Batman; he had been lost.

I thought for a moment. (Yes, it was Tuesday!) I quickly sent out a reply email saying that, unfortunately, we won't know what happened to Batman until Thursday.

I had one fellow teacher who was old enough to get the humor!.

For those of you who are not old enough to get this story, I will explain. The old Batman television show from the 60s used to be shown on Tuesday and Thursday nights. On Tuesday, there was always a horrible cliffhanger that seemed impossible for Batman to escape from. However, he always did!

Getting a Laugh

As I mentioned a little earlier, I was very shy in high school and college.

In one of my first years, we had a staff meeting, and we were role-playing. I don't remember the exact topic, but we were role-playing parents from our school and their interactions with the staff.

This is usually another layer below my comfort level. Just speaking out is one thing, but now adding creativity to that, I was ready to freeze up. It came to my turn, and I had an idea to get out of the assignment in a funny way.

We all had note cards for our lines so the exercise could go in a certain way. I started reading and stumbled over every word.

I stopped, looked at the person sitting next to me, handed her the card, and said, "You're from Powell Valley; you read this." (I insinuated that Powell Valley parents were smarter than the school I was supposed to be from.)

The room erupted with laughter, and it went on and on. I was not used to being someone who could crack up a room and may not have ever felt adrenaline as I did at that moment.

I can see the great feeling that comedians get when everything clicks.

First Day of School

One time, on the first day of school at East Orient, I stepped into the hallway as children and teachers were heading to their classrooms.

I saw a no-nonsense teacher urging a student to her classroom. The student fell to the floor and grabbed her leg, and she dragged him a step or two. His reaction was a little off because he wasn't crying; he seemed to be enjoying this interaction. I stopped him and told him to come sit with me for a while. We stepped into the gym, and I asked him what was wrong.

He said he just didn't want to start school. I told him he was lucky because he had one of the best teachers in the school, and she would make sure that he had a good day. He just couldn't act this way.

I talked him into heading to her class and told him I would check on him at noon. That seemed to do the trick, and at noon, he had settled in. His teacher also assured me he was fine.

Volunteering

After I retired from teaching, I decided I wanted to volunteer a little. I thought that might give me my school fix.

I wanted to volunteer at East Orient, my favorite school. I emailed many of my friends there and explained that I was ready to volunteer but didn't want a regular schedule. If I peeked into their room and they had something for me, great. Otherwise, I would just wander to another room.

One day, I peeked into the no-nonsense teacher's room (mentioned in the previous story). She saw me peeking in her room. I saw her think for just a moment, and then she exclaimed, "YES!" She had to use the restroom and trusted me enough to watch her classroom for a few minutes. It was a win-win for everyone!

The Son of No Nonsense

Here's one more story about this no-nonsense teacher. I worked with her mom at Hall at the very beginning of my career.

She now had several children at East Orient. One day, I was subbing in a 4th-grade classroom, and her son was in it. I would describe her son as one of the most genuinely sincere, helpful students I have ever met.

This happened to be the day before Christmas break, and I subbed in his class for two days.

This student had some duties at the very end of the day. As he was letting me know he was leaving the class, he said, "Merry Christmas, Mr. Rodgers!"

He turned and walked right into a set of lockers.

I eventually asked his mom and grandma if I had a handle on him. I asked them, "Is he the nicest boy ever with a little bit of klutz in him?"

They both laughed out loud and said, "Exactly".

What Time is It?

I was having lunch in the teachers' lounge in my first year. A teacher who you might describe as a little ditzy but who also has a heart of gold was also hurrying into the teachers' lounge.

She exclaimed loudly as she glanced at the microwave across the room, "Who is cooking something for 11 minutes and 40 seconds?"

Everyone's head turned and looked at the microwave. "That's the time, you dork," someone said.

Allergic to Latex

Every year, classroom and PE teachers get health notices for students who might have unusual health concerns. Some of these are very important, especially in PE, where a small bump could be serious for certain students.

One of the most intense health situations was a student who had a latex allergy. I had never heard of this before. This student had several health issues, and we had several meetings concerning this student prior to him entering the school.

I was shocked at how many things latex is in, including the gym floor! The student came to school and had no issues. The staff learned a lot about this students concerns.

Special Education Student

Over the years, I have had many Special Education students. One sticks out in my mind, and one incident was very funny.

This student liked to take off his shoes and toss them around.

One time, a group of students was on the floor, and another teacher was reading them a story. They had their heads down because of something that was happening in the story.

The Special Ed student happened to be walking by and tossed his shoe very high up into the air, right over this group of students.

I was also walking by and got into position to make a catch. I leaned way over the group, stretched out, and caught the shoe.

The funniest part was that the teacher and the group of students still had their heads down, and they had no idea that someone almost got hit by the shoe.

Do I Get Paid for This?

Sometimes, some people just shouldn't work with students. They just don't have the temperament for it.

Years ago, there was an assistant at Hall, and she was one of those people who shouldn't have been in a school. Her work was below par, and she was having a meeting to be put on a Plan of Assistance.

She talked about it openly with other staff members. I remember thinking I would be so embarrassed.

One day, as we were on recess duty, she asked the rest of us, "Will I get paid for the Plan of Assistance meeting?" "I need to check on that."

The Boss of all Teachers

One time, a good friend from my hometown reached out to me. She was in school to study education and needed to do some observations. I was delighted to see my friend, and we set up a time for her to come.

She arrived just as a class was lining up to leave the gym. One student was up to shenanigans, and I called him out on it. My friend was watching from the side.

Always ready and looking to get a laugh, I pointed at my friend and said to my student, "Do you know who that is? She is the boss of all teachers. She is here to make sure students are behaving themselves and teachers are doing a good job."

This bewildered my student and my friend. However, I was getting a kick out of my humor, which was the most important thing.

Playing Hooky (Not Hockey)

One time, I was in Las Vegas, and it was a school day. I was in a casino and was going through a doorway. I nearly bumped into a person, stepped back, and excused myself.

The person I nearly bumped into was a colleague from Gresham. She laughed and said, "What are you doing here on a school day?"

I said, "I'm playing hooky; what are you doing here?" She said, "I'm here on union business", she deadpanned.

"Sure", I said.

Another time, I was headed somewhere on a Thursday night. I headed toward my gate, and waiting at the gate next to mine was an entire family from my school.

I laughed and said, "You caught me; it looks like I am playing hooky tomorrow!"

What's for Lunch

One day, as I was walking down the ramp into the lunchroom, I saw a student who was turned toward the wall and crying.

Now, students get free breakfast and lunch, but you had to pay for lunch at this time.

This 2nd-grade boy was out of money and didn't know what to do or how to advocate for himself for some food. I talked to him and asked him what was wrong. He told me he was out of money and hated peanut butter. (That was the free option).

I talked to the lunch lady. Now, lunchtime is an incredibly busy time for the servers. I explained that this student had no money and hated peanut butter. Wasn't there anything else that we could do?

Finally, we wrangled a hot dog and a fruit cup, and he was happy.

I left that duty feeling very good. Some people might think this is a self-serving story.

Someone on the staff would have made this story have a good ending. I just felt that, in this instance, we did right by the student. It wasn't his fault that there was no money in his account. I was happy that we didn't let him fall through the cracks. It was such a little thing for us but such a big hurdle for that second grader.

A Family of Teachers

During my first few years at Hall, I met a fellow teacher who became a very good friend.

That first year, I was playing a city league basketball game when I saw an acquaintance from college on the other team.

We guarded each other, and he was a very physical player. We pushed and played very hard. When the action stopped, we would visit.

"I teach at Hall in Gresham," I said. "My sister teaches at Hall," he said. We both agreed that his sister was a wonderful person and teacher.

As I got to know her better, I learned she came from a very big family, and most of her family were teachers. Her husband was a teacher, and her kids would grow up to be teachers. Even the kid their family would take in as they were growing up became a teacher.

Oh, and a great sidenote…She taught NBA Player Damon Stoudamire when he was a youngster.

This is the Best Class Ever!

When I was at Hall, I was scheduled to teach Adaptive PE with the regular PE teacher, so there were two PE teachers for this class.

One day, the PE teacher and I were walking down the hall to class, and we saw some people from the District Office waiting for us. They were there to observe this class, along with some other Special Ed teachers doing an observation.

I felt we always did a quality job teaching this class, but to be honest, there wasn't a lot of prior preparation.

Walking down that hall, realizing we had visitors, Craig said, "Oh Oh—let's do this for this class."

One sentence prepped us for the class, and we kept the students busy and engaged.

At the end of the class, the visitors complimented us on having one of the most well-organized and well-run classes they had ever seen.

I don't know if having two certified PE teachers made the difference. Craig and I often laughed, at least on that occasion, at just how much preparation went into the class.

Unaware Principal

One time, I had a principal who started meetings by saying, "It is 8:00. Let's start our meeting." I imagine it was his way of instilling punctuality in his staff.

One time, a teacher came into our meeting just a couple of minutes late, and the principal stopped the meeting and asked her why she was late.

She replied, "Traffic was bad."

He said, "Maybe you should have left a little earlier to take it into account."

Now, I imagine this principal had a point to make about punctuality. In making that point, he lost a lot of respect and trust in his staff.

Hindsight is always great. I like to think I would have said something that would have made that principal feel about two feet tall. Something like, I had a relative pass this morning, so yes, I am running late.

Same Principal

During my last few years of teaching, I had a hip problem, and I was eventually in need of a hip replacement.

When I first learned of the problem, I sat down with this principal just to let him know so he wasn't unaware. I wasn't ready to schedule surgery yet; this was just a heads-up.

His comment started to tell me that when the time came, I should think about scheduling the surgery in the summer so I wouldn't miss too much school.

He must have realized how inappropriate this was because he backed off his statement.

Sure, I am ready for hip replacement in October, but I will just wait until closer to summer.

It's Snowing!!!!!

There are always a lot of things that go on inside a school. However, there is one thing that makes a school buzz like nothing else...snow.

If there ever is a day when the kids have to go home earlier than planned due to snow, the school literally becomes a madhouse.

Every parent has to be called to check on plans and connections. If the student is riding home on the bus, will there be adults home at that time? Do parents have to make alternate plans in any way? Are there different people picking up the students, etc.?

Then the buses need to be checked. School buses and drivers run on many routes in a day. Are they available, and will they be on time? This is another process in which families and the public do not know what is involved.

Health Program

When I was at East Orient, the principal informed me that I would be teaching a canned Health Program, like a watered-down version of DARE.

The program focused on making good choices and brain development, along with a few other concepts.

These lessons were taught approximately once a month in place of a PE lesson. For most students, this was like expecting a hot fudge sundae (PE) and getting liver (Health).

I don't remember one time when I heard a student say, "Hooray, Today, we are having Health!"

Here is the strange thing: I really liked teaching this program. I liked teaching in the classroom. They had good activities and set up good discussions, and usually, the kids were engaged quickly and didn't complain too much about missing PE.

Interviewing for Assistants

After going through a lot of interviews to get a job, it was very interesting to be on the other side of the table, interviewing for my library assistant position at Hall.

I had a chance to do this process twice. It was interesting because I knew most of the people that we interviewed and had positive thoughts on all of them. Some of them interviewed well, and for a couple, it was painful as you could literally see their brain freeze up.

The first decision went to a person who was probably overqualified. A former teacher who had moved and was getting accredited after her move.

After two years, that person left to sub, hoping to get a regular teaching job.

In the second session, the person hired interviewed the best and, on paper, was not one of the favorites. This person happened to be the school's cook. However, she did a great job and, after Media Specialists were eliminated, ran the library at Hall for twenty years.

Picking Teams

You could almost write a book on the art of picking, dividing, or making teams.

Gone are the days of the old schoolyard when two captains were choosing teams.

There are so many ways to make teams. One of the easiest is to line the class up and then count them off. The students will often try to arrange themselves so they can still get on the team with their friends.

Sometimes, I like to say get back-to-back with a classmate. You will not be on the same team with this classmate. Then there are so many ways to divide them.

Taller people on this team, shorter people on that team. Whose birthday comes first? They are on that team. Darker shirts were on that team, and lighter-colored ones were on that team. Longer hair on that team means shorter hair on that team.

I remember I did Captain's Choice one time, but I added a wrinkle. I whispered to the captains that they were choosing the other captain's team. If they told anyone, they would have to keep the team they chose. So, in theory, the students who are usually chosen last in this game are chosen first.

This caused a ruckus in the class, as the students could not figure out what was happening. I like the idea of this, but the students questioned it too much.

Potlatch

Many years ago, at Hall, the 4th grade had an evening event called Potlatch. Potlatch was a Native American "giving ceremony."

To go along with that I had been to an author signing and had books for some of the very top students.

One of the students I had a book for was such a helpful student. She was best friends with a blind girl and she was literally the eyes for this girl.

As I walked to the microphone and composed what I would say, I thought, "Do not say we have a blind girl here at Hall as a way to start my introduction."

I started, "We have a blind girl here at Hall."...(In mind my, I am saying NO, that was not how I was supposed to start this.) There was only one blind girl at Hall, and she started coming forward. I had to somehow say no; the book was for the blind girl's friend, in one of the most cringing moments of my career.

Student Council

Another of my duties at East Orient was being in charge of the Student Council. Each 4th and 5th grade class voted on a representative for the student council.

Student Council would oversee reading the daily announcements over the intercom, take part in assemblies, and help the school in other ways. I always enjoyed working with these students.

Janitor

All the janitors I worked with were great. However, there were times when students would either bleed or perhaps get sick.

I would always feel bad when I had to call on the walkie-talkie for a janitor because it was not a nice job. One janitor always replied that it was job security!

Best Invention Ever

I really think Libraries are the best inventions ever. Where else can you get something, use it, and then return it so the next person can use it?

When I was a Media Specialist, my strongest trait was my ability to understand what students really liked to read about.

One of my favorite activities was talking about books in a way that would interest students and get them to check them out.

I loved ordering books like Bird Eating Spiders. Holy crap, who isn't going to be interested in that. Even the girls were fascinated. When doing lessons like that, I always tried to include many different types of books to hook everyone's interests.

A third-grade teacher once told me that third-grade boys generally don't want to read fiction; they want to read about real things like cars, animals, and bulldozers. Now I know that is a generality.

At that time, students loved Goosebumps, American Girls, and Boxcar Children, along with picture books that showcased humor.

Principal Video

One year, our principal was injured in a car accident. The school was making a video for her.

I wrote a quick song and went to a 3rd-grade class. It was to the theme of WE WILL ROCK YOU, retitled to We Will Miss You.

I got the class to do that easy beat. Then I sang the lyrics and had the class sing We Will, We will Miss You.

I remember one line the kids loved; “Reading, Writing, ‘Rithmatic, it’s enough to make us sick!

The Parents Are In the Room

Teaching is really a job that is full of responsibility. Over the years, I have had parent inquiries about things that have happened in my class.

Sometimes, I had no idea what they were talking about; I had no knowledge of the incident.

Other times, I knew what the parent was talking about, and at the time, it seemed like such a small thing that was really blown out of proportion.

At any rate, it made me think and start to react to situations quicker and not let them fester.

I started taking a mindset that all the parents were on the sidelines watching the class. Would they leave happy with the class and how their child fit in, or would they be unhappy with how their student was treated or the amount of activity they received?

There isn't any way to make everyone happy, but I think you can do your best to ensure students are not unjustly treated. That is a tough one for a class where there is so much movement and so much going on.

Reading Competitions

When I was a Media Specialist, several times, I came up with competitions to help promote reading.

One year, I told the kids that the school would try to read one million pages. I had slips available for students, and when they read a book, they listed their name, the book's title, the number of pages, and a parent or teacher's initials.

I didn't really think it through; this was a year-long project. There was a lot of work on this project. Students ended up reading over 334,000 pages. We had a small write-up in the Gresham paper.

Another of my favorite competitions was an Iditarod dog sled race. The premise was the same, the more students read, the more their sled moved. It was a competition that we did for two weeks.

A few teachers objected to The Iditarod theme as it can be cruel to dogs. So, during the assembly, we mentioned that.

Author Letters

Another of my favorite activities for library class was writing to authors and hoping they would write back.

I had addresses for a good number of authors, and I would spend one class presenting their choices. They would choose who they were going to write.

The following class, as a group, would write the letter. I had a guide for them on things they could ask. The class was always a little indifferent when writing the letter. However, when the letters started coming back, it was very exciting.

For the authors, it was a win-win situation. They could promote their work and reach possible readers. Several would really go out of their way to provide a very personal letter.

Tag Games

Tag games are always popular. The key is to change the games so there are different ways to play tag and give students a chance to be creative.

One of my favorite games was cartoon tag. Three people are "it." Each one chooses a cartoon. Then, the remaining students get to choose one of the three cartoons, and they will run when theirs is chosen. For safety, this spreads out the game, so not so many are running at one time.

Zombie tag is also popular. The people who are it are zombies, and everyone must lumber around just the way zombies do. Kids love this because they are moving, and it lets them create.

There are hundreds of ways to play tag; the most important thing is that it gets kids moving.

Fight, Fight, Fight

Fights in elementary school are really few and far between. Nothing much usually happens. There are exceptions.

There is one fight I remember. A class came into the gym, and I don't know what occurred, but one boy, who I would describe as a very nice, well-mannered young man, started fighting with the class troublemaker.

They were both very upset. The classroom teacher came in, and I said, almost apologetically, "I have to send them both." I called the nice boy over and told him to just tell his story, and it should be OK.

Rules have now been changed to probable suspensions for anyone fighting.

Clothes Pin Game

Another of my favorite 2-minute games was called the Clothes Pin game. The class stood on a line, and everyone closed their eyes. I went behind them and hooked the clothespin to someone's clothing. I always tried my best to put it somewhere that was a challenge to find.

They then opened their eyes and tried to find the clothespin. The only rule I had was if they found the clothespin, just raise their hand. Try not to follow the person around who had the clothespin. That told everyone you found it. That way, other people could continue to play.

Unique Stories

Miscellaneous and Unique Stories

After seeing approximately 8,000 students, you can be sure there were some unique students and some unique stories.

One student just didn't talk. He didn't talk kindergarten through 5th grade. Well, he didn't talk at school; according to his parents, he talked up a storm at home.

One girl walked on her tiptoes the entire time I saw her in school. Someone thought perhaps she spent too much time in a walker.

One student in kindergarten would fall during his warmups every day. He was popular, and all the kids would rush to check on him. It was like clockwork. I just think he liked the attention.

One time, I shared media classes with another teacher. She often used puppets to teach her class. I walked through the edge of her class. She was teaching a 5th-grade class, and puppets weren't the approach I would have taken.

As I walked through, I caught the eye of a sharp 5th-grade girl who rolled her eyes. I laughed to myself as I walked on.

Flashbacks to my first grade in 1966.

In first grade, I was initially placed in a class where I seemed to excel. After about three weeks, I switched to a different class.

Even in first grade, I could tell this class was where the neat kids were. Years later, I realized the classes were ability-based. I just recognized that neat kids were in this particular class, the next neat in that class, etc.

I went from a classroom where I was flourishing to a classroom where I was struggling and even had to stay in for recess because my work wasn't done.

Another couple of weeks went by, and I was switched to another classroom. This classroom appeared to be just right ability-wise.

One day, the principal and two other men came into our classroom. They moved to one boy and asked him to grab his things, and they took him out of the room.

The teacher waited a minute and said, "Billy doesn't take baths."

No one really said anything, but even as a first-grader, I thought she should be telling us this?

I don't remember the backlash on Billy when he returned, but that was a moment from the 60's.

During this class, I remember we had to sit up in front of the class and read out loud from the reading book.

I remember that I missed one word all the time I read aloud. The word I missed was "another". I think the sentence read; I want another cracker. I stammered over 'another' and said 'animal' several times. When the teacher gave me the word, I nearly burst into tears.

Bus Evacuation

Once a year, schools have bus evacuation drills. This drill is designed for students to learn what to do in an emergency. They learn the escape doors and how to utilize them. They learn what they could do if the driver ever becomes incapacitated.

The most interesting thing I noticed was how the bus drivers spoke to the students. Knowing they are not trained to talk to students, their exchanges at times are rough.

Sometimes, I have seen teachers intervene to help smooth the way. It makes you realize drivers are paid to drive and not teach students.

Principals

I believe I had twelve principals in my career. Remember, at times, I was working at two different schools.

The day I met one principal, he was having a horrible day. He was grumpy, tired, and, truth be told, a little unpleasant that day. It turns out it was just a bad day, and he was one of the better principals I had.

He had a message for the teachers on the work days before the year started: "This is your job; what goes on inside these walls is your job. "What goes on outside of these walls is your life. "Don't ever let your job interfere with your life."

He said something similar yearly, and I always looked forward to hearing that. It wasn't a message that any other principal ever came close to relaying. It was definitely appreciated.

Last Day of School

You think students love the last day of school? Let me tell you a secret. The students have nothing on the teachers regarding the excitement level.

One of the teacher's greatest challenges is to manage that last day. You throw in just a little bit of learning so you can call it school.

You throw in some cleaning because that helps the teacher as well. You have a party or a celebration. You mix in an extra recess.

Then, you lead them out to the bus. At East Orient, the tradition was that the teachers all did the Can-Can dance as the students drove away.

This is part of the cycle that continues over and over for a teacher. People quickly point out the perk that teachers get summers off, which is nice.

People must understand it takes a short period of time for teachers to decompress so they can relax. Then, just about the time teachers hit relaxation mode, they see the first Back To School Sale ads. I am slow to anger, but Back to School ads are the closest thing that gets me to furious mode.

Then, towards the end of the summer, teachers start to gear up for the new challenge. Teachers definitely need summers!

Top Teachers

I wanted to highlight several teachers that I worked with, and I struggled about just blatantly heaping praise on someone. Then, this book was almost done, and I hadn't included anything of what I really wanted to say about them. So, this is how I want to handle it. I will describe these two teachers and try to capture what made them valuable to a school.

This teacher was a 4th grade teacher at Hall. I worked with her for ten years. I think nearly every teacher I ever worked with was a dedicated teacher. There are just a few that come with a little extra.

At the end of the day, this teacher always had students yearning to spend more time with her. They would stay after school to "help" or to get extra time. I never saw this teacher turn down that extra time to spend with students.

She provided an atmosphere in her class that was welcoming and fun. As a teacher, I would go to her class during party time. I knew that was the place to be in the building.

I'm not saying she was perfect. I remember she had a student who may have been the toughest student I ever saw in my career. Undoubtedly, he was headed to a rough life once school was over.

During the year, he moved from her class to another school. I still remember her last day with him; as she walked back to her classroom, she let out a war hoop of elation.

But you know what? She gave him 100% every day that he was in her class.

When my niece was going into education and needed observation time, I sent her to this teacher.

Oh, by the way, my niece is now a principal. The little overachiever!

The second teacher I want to mention is one who taught music at East Orient. Again, maybe the most positive person on the face of the earth.

She was a person that the kids gravitated to. I was always amazed listening to her interact with kids. She found something positive to say in nearly every conversation. It wasn't forced, it was genuine. That's what the kids pick up on.

I have seen her get cross a few times as she worked under the pressure of putting on a school concert and the details that it encompasses. Even then, it is half the frustration I would have shown.

She is someone that I, as an adult, gravitated to because she would always make me feel better.

When I was unexpectedly transferred from East Orient, I told this teacher the news. She grabbed me in a hug that told me I was her friend and that I would be missed. That hug just went on and on. I still remember it to this day.

These teachers lent stories of their own to share.

Rich Owen Story #1

Rich was teaching at Boring Middle School, and a student got in trouble and was given in-school suspension. This student's mother was contacted, and she objected to the plan being put in place for her son. She didn't want him sleeping or reading or even doing homework.

Mom showed up the next day at school with trash-picking-up equipment. Mom followed him around every day after school. It was a genuine commitment by mom to follow up on discipline.

Rich Owen Story #2

Rich had taught one year at Boring Middle School, and towards the end of the year, the school had to follow a RIFT process, as a teacher would lose their job.

Rich and another teacher were hired on the same day, and the RIFT process was between these two teachers. It was finally decided that the decision was to be made by drawing straws.

Rich got the short straw, but this story has a good ending, as he goes on to teach at David Douglas High School.

Rich Owen Story #3

Rich taught 7th-grade math, and he struggled to fill the time allotted to the class. They would correct papers, study new concepts, and even have time to work on the new assignment. If there was time left in class, he decided to go out and shoot some baskets with his class as a reward.

On one occasion, they were out shooting, and the principal wandered by. Rich was a little hesitant, not knowing if the principal would object to him bringing the class out to shoot baskets. The principal walked by Rich, put his hand on his shoulder, and simply said to Rich, "I understand."

Dean Jackson works at a preschool auditory center.

One of his students was driving past in a pedal toy and stuck his head out the window and said to Dean, "Mr. Biddles is no more." Dean had no idea what that meant or where it came from.

Michelle Trapas Story

When I first started teaching at East Orient, I had been out of elementary school for years. I wanted to get to know what the kids were interested in, how to tap into what they were naturally excited about.

I invited several kids from each of the 3rd, 4th, and 5th grades to have lunch with me on Fridays. They could bring their lunch into the music room, and they could share jokes or stories, special skills, or events that they wanted to talk about. Most talked about their sports teams or places they had gone on vacation with their families.

Some would proudly do a cartwheel that they had finally mastered. One 5th grader, however, was a quiet, reserved sort of kid. He sat listening and observing most of the lunchtime.

About 15 minutes into our 20 minutes together, he offered a comment: "I can stand on my hands." I quickly asked him to show us. He stood up and put his hands underneath his shoes. We all laughed, and I was surprised to find out that he had such a quirky sense of humor.

Warming to his audience, he then said, "I can pour this chocolate milk up my nose and make it come out of my eyes." Well, of course, we all wanted to see how he would fool us this time.

Nope. He actually tipped the carton of chocolate milk, so the spout poured about a tablespoon of chocolate milk into his upturned nostril. Then, he held his breath, and sure enough, a chocolate tear trickled down his cheek from one eye!

All his peers and I watched, mouths agape, not understanding what we were seeing. A few laughed nervously, but most of us were stunned. After that lunch, I rarely allowed a student to share their special skills with me unless I had a clear idea of what they were doing!

Kathy Thorn's Story

Kathy told this story to me recently. She taught 2nd grade at North. She had a new student who she greeted. She put her hand on his shoulder. He respectfully asked that she not touch him. He didn't like to be touched.

She glanced through his records and saw that he was on the spectrum, which was no problem for a veteran like her. They made it through the year and were headed out to the bus for the last time.

This student was the last one in line to get on the bus. As the other students had boarded, he turned around and gave Mrs. Thorne a big hug and said that he loved her!

Betsy Wilcox story

When someone said, "I can't do it!" I would break into song and sing the song from Cinderella... "It's possible". The kids loved it!!! Always put a smile on their faces...whether they liked it or not or thought it was funny...changed their attitude towards their frustrations.

Colleen Adams Story. (The Boss of All Teachers)

I could tell you about teaching online during COVID-19, only to see one of my third graders showing us all his private parts. I turned off his camera before anyone else saw, but I was scarred for life!!

Craig Hemenway Story

I was on duty at recess one day when a fourth grader came up and told me that Billy had hit him, and it really hurt. I called Billy over and asked him if it was true that he punched the other student. He said yes, it was true.

I asked him why, and he said it was because Justin had hit him first. So, then I questioned Justin again and asked if this was the truth? His reply was yes, I hit him first, but Billy had hit him much harder, and it really hurt. I sent both boys away with a warning to play nice. I figured the lesson was learned.

Final Bell

It's time to go home…Final Bell

No matter how much you liked school as a student or a teacher, there was always that great feeling of the day being done when you heard that final bell.

School...almost everyone has some fond memories of school. Be it a favorite teacher, the comradery of a friendship, and the activities you did together, success in an assignment or a specific class.

Thinking back on all the teachers I have worked with, I realize they are an amazing group of people. Each one carries a certain strength that will be able to somehow engage students.

I have seen the young, cool, male teacher that resonates with the students. Each student wants to be close to this teacher to get his attention. He is thoughtful and outgoing.

I have seen the quiet male teacher who relies on expectations and humor to grab the attention of his students.

I have seen the most wonderfully sweet, grandmotherly type of teacher who dearly loves each student and finds the positives and connection with each student.

I have said on my journey that I knew I had to struggle with discipline because I think kids saw that I was a kind person. Truth be told, they could probably get away with a couple of things.

As I have said before, I know I can teach. I feel I have a way to reach students and impart information.

Hopefully, these stories will bring forth memories of your school adventures. Perhaps you will get a sense of how schools have changed. Perhaps it will give you a new appreciation for teachers and the job they do.

Mike with son Zach at Harvard

About the Author

Born in Port Angeles, Washington, in 1960, Mike Rodger's journey has been marked by a passion for education and storytelling. He spent his early years in Seaside, Oregon, living with his mother and grandparents. A love of reading, sparked by time spent in rural Ohio and Maryland, profoundly shaped his childhood. Inspired by both positive and challenging experiences with physical education teachers, Mike pursued a degree in PE, studying at Mt. Hood Community College and Western Oregon State College before completing his training at Portland State University as a Media Specialist.

Throughout an expansive teaching career, primarily at Hall Elementary School in Gresham, Oregon, Mike demonstrated a commitment to nurturing and inspiring students. A lifelong learner, he also explored journalism through wrestling—a subject close to his heart. For three decades, he published *Ring Around The Northwest*, a wrestling bulletin featuring interviews, history, and insights into the sport. This passion culminated in books like *Excitement In The Air (3 volumes)*, *Katie Bar The Door*, and *The Encyclopedia of Portland Wrestling*, all chronicling the rich history of Pacific Northwest wrestling. He also chronicled the history of wrestling in Hawaii in "*Ohhh Yeahhh*". Mike has also refereed, provided commentary, and even stepped into the ring, bringing an unparalleled depth to his knowledge of wrestling and storytelling. In 2019, Mike received the prestigious James Melby Wrestling Historian of the Year Award.

Above: Mike after a grueling match as a referee
Below: Mike interviews Playboy Buddy Rose

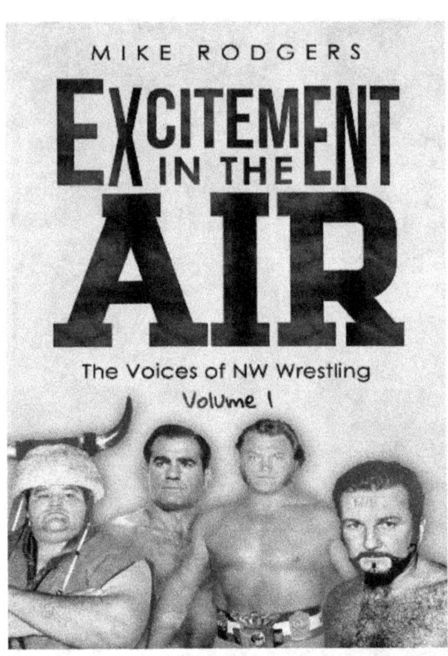
MIKE RODGERS
EXCITEMENT IN THE AIR
The Voices of NW Wrestling
Volume 1

MIKE RODGERS
EXCITEMENT IN THE AIR
The Voices of NW Wrestling
Volume 2

MIKE RODGERS
EXCITEMENT IN THE AIR
The Voices of NW Wrestling
Volume 2

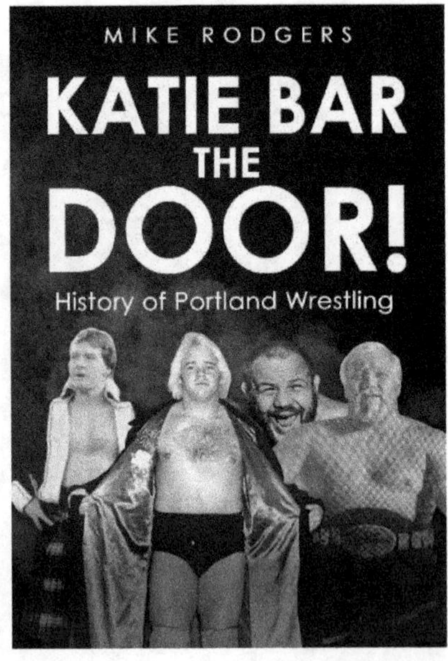
MIKE RODGERS
KATIE BAR THE DOOR!
History of Portland Wrestling

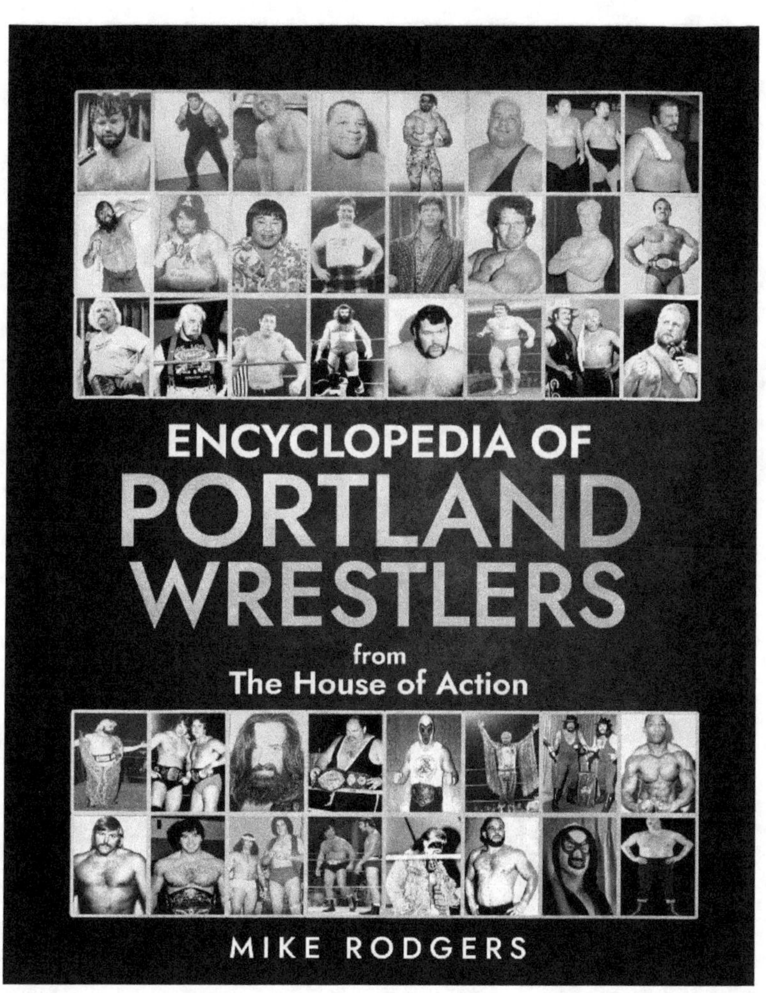
ENCYCLOPEDIA OF
PORTLAND
WRESTLERS
from
The House of Action
MIKE RODGERS

Ohhh Yeahhh
History of Hawaiian Wrestling